Fewer, Clearer, Higher

HARVARD EDUCATION LETTER

IMPACT SERIES

The *Harvard Education Letter* Impact Series offers an in-depth look at timely topics in education. Individual volumes explore current trends in research, practice, and policy. The series brings many voices into the conversation about issues in contemporary education and considers reforms from the perspective of—and on behalf of—educators in the field.

OTHER BOOKS IN THIS SERIES

I Used to Think . . . And Now I Think . . .
Edited by Richard F. Elmore

Inside School Turnarounds
Laura Pappano

Something in Common
Robert Rothman

From Data to Action
Edited by Milbrey McLaughlin
and Rebecca A. London

Fewer, Clearer, Higher

How the Common Core State Standards Can Change Classroom Practice

ROBERT ROTHMAN

HARVARD EDUCATION PRESS
CAMBRIDGE, MASSACHUSETTS

KH

HARVARD EDUCATION LETTER
IMPACT SERIES

Library of Congress Control Number 2013941193
Paperback ISBN 978-1-61250-619-7
Library Edition ISBN 978-1-61250-620-3

Published by Harvard Education Press,
an imprint of the Harvard Education Publishing Group

Harvard Education Press
8 Story Street
Cambridge, MA 02138

Cover Design: Ciano Design
The typefaces used in this book are Sabon and Frutiger

9/30/15

Contents

Preface

A 2012 survey of mathematics teachers by William Schmidt of Michigan State University found some good news and bad news for supporters of the Common Core State Standards. The good news was that the vast majority of teachers had read the Standards and liked them. The bad news was that 80 percent of the teachers considered the Standards "pretty much the same" as their state standards.

The fact is that the Standards in many ways call for substantial departures from current practice. For example, they propose a sharp increase in the use of informational text in English language arts and a balance between procedural knowledge, conceptual understanding, and problem-solving in mathematics. Both of these ideas represent a significant change from the way those subjects are taught in large numbers of classrooms. The title of this book, *Fewer, Clearer, Higher,* taken from the mantra used by the standards writers in their efforts to craft the Common Core, suggests that the Standards were intended to contrast sharply from previous standards.

A good deal of the effort to support the implementation of the Common Core Standards has focused on underscoring the distinctions between the Standards and conventional practice. For example, Student Achievement Partners, an organization founded by the lead writers of the Standards, has developed a set of videos and documents describing the "instructional shifts" the Standards call for.

The message might be starting to sink in. A survey of teachers conducted a year after Schmidt's survey found that teachers felt unprepared to teach the Standards. Asked to rate their readiness on a scale of 1 to 5, with 5 indicating "very prepared," half the teachers rated themselves a 3 or below.[1]

These findings suggest that there is a strong need among teachers to understand the Common Core State Standards more deeply, including the rationale for them and what they imply for instruction. That's what this book attempts to do. Let me be clear about what it is not: this is not a "how-to" book. There are no lesson plans or templates, no rubrics or checklists. There are many other books that offer much more practical guidance than *Fewer, Clearer, Higher.*

Instead, this book tries to help people make sense of the Standards, from the point of view of an observer who has followed their development and implementation fairly closely. The book tries to explain why the Standards writers took the approach they did, with research where appropriate; what the Standards say; and what these changes look like when implemented. To a great extent, I have relied on actual examples from classrooms, using references to videos and other resources that teachers can check out for more information. I have included a list of some of the most important resources for teachers in the appendix.

As my previous book, *Something in Common: The Common Core Standards and the Next Chapter in American Education,* tried to make clear, I believe the Standards have the strong potential to transform teaching and learning and help bring about the kind of deeper learning that will be increasingly important for all young people. I stated in that book that there are three aspects of the Common Core State Standards that distinguish them from previous standards efforts, which had a modest effect on student learning. First, the Standards are clear and coherent, and teachers who have read them overwhelmingly support them and say they represent what they should be teaching. There is less likelihood for indifference or resistance, a problem that plagued the standards efforts of the 1990s.

Second, the state consortia developing assessments to measure student performance against the Standards are working closely with the standards writers to ensure that the assessments actually assess what the Standards intend. This, too, would represent a change from the 1990s, when many state tests veered from the standards, and teachers, quite understandably, focused on what was tested rather than on what the standards suggested.

And third, the fact that the Common Core State Standards have been adopted by forty-six states and the District of Columbia has made possible cross-state implementation efforts and national efforts that could not have happened when each state developed its own standards. The commonness of the Common Core has made many institutions, from teacher-education programs to commercial publishers, sit up and take notice.

Nevertheless, I am under no illusions that the Standards will, in and of themselves, transform instruction and learning. As the teachers' doubts make clear, implementing the Standards will require substantial learning for teachers, and states and districts vary widely in the amount of support they are providing. A key step in learning to change to what the Standards expect is getting a clear picture of what the Standards say and why their authors took the approach they did. I hope this book contributes to that understanding.

How to Use This Book

Fewer, Clearer, Higher provides a detailed look at the Common Core State Standards and the changes in classroom practice they call for. It explains in depth the content of the Standards and their specific implications for instructional practice, contrasting these implications with traditional practices. And it includes descriptions of lessons aligned with the Standards, as well as examples of assessment tasks designed to measure student performance against the Standards.

I have organized the book around nine aspects of the Standards that make them distinct from much of contemporary practice: four in mathematics, which are discussed in chapters 2 through 5, and five in English language arts, discussed in chapters 6 through 10. While these nine features are unique, they are related to one another. For example, the focus in the mathematics standards makes possible in-depth instruction that allows for teaching procedural fluency, conceptual understanding, and problem-solving. Likewise, the emphasis in the English language arts standards on the use of evidence is a key feature of the standards for speaking and listening. That's because the Standards represent a coherent vision of what students should know and be able to do at every grade level.

In many cases, I quote directly from the Common Core State Standards as published by the National Governors Association and the Council of Chief State School Officers (www.corestandards.org) in 2010. In those documents, the English language arts standards are organized around a set of "anchor standards" in reading, writing, language, and speaking and listening, which are common for all grades. The mathematics standards differ from grade to grade. The notations by the Standards I cite refer to the original documents; some states that have adopted the Standards might have reorganized them since their initial publication.

Chapter 1 briefly outlines the development of the Common Core State Standards to provide context for the rest of the book. It describes the factors that led to the initiative, the process that the standards writers used to develop the Standards, and efforts under way to implement them. It also describes plans for assessments that are being developed to measure student performance against the Standards.

Chapter 2, "Less Is More," shows how the Common Core Standards focus on a few key topics and expect students to master them in depth. This represents a sharp departure from many prior state standards, which tended to include a lot of topics, leading to the charge that mathematics education in the United States was "a mile wide and an inch deep." The chapter describes some of the tradeoffs necessary to achieve focus, such as deferring standards on data and statistics until grade six.

Chapter 3, "Achieving Coherence," discusses how the Standards achieve the "clearer" goal by building in a coherent sequence of expectations for each grade level. The coherence is achieved in two ways. First, there is coherence within a grade level; topics are joined in ways that make sense mathematically and that make it easier for teachers to teach them effectively. In addition, the Standards attempt to chart a logical progression of student learning across years, so that student knowledge and skills build on prior learning.

Chapter 4, "An End to the Math Wars," shows how the Standards represent a truce in the long-running battle between those who have argued that mathematics instruction should focus on student proficiency in mathematics procedures and those who have argued for an emphasis on conceptual understanding. Both are essential, the Standards state. Thus there are clear expectations that students should demonstrate fluency in procedures (such as a knowledge of multiplication tables), show an understanding of the concepts that underlie basic mathematics principles (for example, explain why two fractions are equivalent), and be able to apply their knowledge to solve real-world problems.

Chapter 5, "Covering All the Bases," describes the eight mathematical practices that accompany the content standards in the Common Core. These practices, as the Standards document describes them, are the "varieties of expertise that mathematics educators at all levels should seek to develop in their students."

Turning to changes in English language arts instruction, chapter 6, "Just the Facts," shows that the Standards call for a substantially higher proportion of nonfiction reading than schools typically assign: 50 percent in elementary school and 70 percent in high school. These proportions, the document states, reflect the fact that students will read primarily nonfiction after high school.

Chapter 7, "Prove It," examines the Standards' emphasis on the use of evidence. This emphasis is prominent in the standards for reading, writing, and speaking. In reading, the standards call for students to demonstrate the ability to read closely and use a text to support conclusions. In writing, students are expected to "write arguments to support claims . . . using relevant and sufficient evidence." In speaking, students should "present information, findings, and supporting evidence such that listeners can follow the line of reasoning."

Chapter 8, "Up the Staircase," examines the requirement that students demonstrate the ability to read and comprehend increasingly complex texts. The Standards document cites research showing that understanding complex texts is one of the most important factors in college and career readiness. However, while the complexity of texts used in postsecondary education and the workplace has remained steady, there is evidence that the complexity of texts in high schools has declined over the past forty years.

Chapter 9, "Elevating Discussion," looks specifically at the standards for speaking and listening. The fact that the document includes standards for these abilities is itself new; state standards rarely included them as part of English language arts. Yet the document notes that oral language is integral to literacy.

Chapter 10, "A Role for Everyone," focuses on the standards for literacy in the content areas. In addition to the English language arts standards of reading, writing, language, and speaking and listening, the Common Core Standards include standards for literacy in science, social studies, and technical subjects. These are based on the idea that literacy in each disciplinary area is unique, and that the ability to, say, read and comprehend a historical document is integral to learning history. At the same time, these standards are also based on a recognition that all teachers, not just English teachers, are responsible for developing students' literacy abilities.

Finally, chapter 11, "The Road Ahead," offers a cautionary note. It looks at the hurdles ahead for implementation and discusses the major steps that need to happen at the state and national levels to ensure that the Standards achieve their goal of improving instruction and learning. While these hurdles are significant, there is considerable activity under way that provides some hope.

And there is a great deal of hope riding on the Standards. For the first time, nearly the entire nation has agreed on what students should know and be able to do, and has tied those expectations to evidence about what students need to learn in order to succeed in college and careers. That is a huge step. Realizing that goal might not be easy, but it is worth the effort. It is time to make it happen.

CHAPTER

1

The Common Core State Standards and the Next Chapter in American Education

Educators in the United States are now engaged in an unprecedented effort to redefine what students are expected to know and be able to do. This effort is particularly remarkable because, for the first time, nearly all states have adopted the same standards for student performance. These standards, known as the Common Core State Standards, have the potential to transform teaching and learning in almost every classroom in the country.

States have been setting standards for what students should know and be able to do for two decades. But the Common Core State Standards represent a sea change, for a number of reasons. First, the Standards were intended to be common across states—that is, they were designed to abolish the wide variations in standards among states and to ensure that all students would be held to the same expectations, regardless of where they happened to live. Second, the Standards were crafted explicitly to lead to college and career readiness for students, which was not always the goal under standards adopted previously. Policy makers and educators were concerned that under the pre–Common Core system, students in many states could meet their states' standards, yet find themselves, after high school, unprepared for higher education or the workplace. The Common Core State Standards were written to match the expectations of postsecondary learning. And third, the Common Core Standards were created as the centerpiece of a redesign of state education systems. Shortly after the release of the Standards, the federal government awarded $330 million to two consortia of states to develop new, ambitious assessments to measure student performance against the Standards. Because of the strong influence of tests on instruction, these assessments are likely to encourage schools and teachers to focus on the Standards. At the same time, curriculum developers and professional development organizations are redesigning products and services around the Common Core State Standards.

How did it happen that nearly every state agreed to adopt the same standards for students? This chapter will describe briefly the movement that led to the creation of the Standards, the process the standards writers went through to draft them, and the actions that were taken by states to adopt them and begin their implementation.

Standards and American Education

States and school districts have long defined what students should study. Usually these definitions have consisted of graduation requirements mandating that students take a prescribed number of courses in particular subjects in order to earn a diploma. However, these requirements typically said little about the content that all students should learn.

In the 1980s, though, research in cognitive science and in educational policy converged around the idea of setting clear standards for what students should know and be able to do, and of using these standards as the fulcrum of educational systems. Cognitive researchers found that students learn best when the expectations for their learning are clear and when they can set targets for their own improvement. Policy researchers found that education policy could become more coherent and effective if it centered on clear standards for student performance, with assessments, curriculum, and professional development aligned to those standards.[1]

Building on those ideas, subject-matter organizations, led by the National Council of Teachers of Mathematics (NCTM), decided to spell out the specific content and skills necessary for all students. The NCTM standards, released in a 1989 document titled *Curriculum and Evaluation Standards for School Mathematics,* outlined a set of topics that in many ways represented a significant shift for many schools. The document proved enormously influential, at least initially, both in schools and with other subject-matter organizations representing English, science, and social studies teachers. By one estimate, the NCTM standards were used as a model by forty states in revising curricula and helped inform the redesign of tests, such as the National Assessment of Educational Progress (NAEP).[2] The document also helped inspire other subject-matter organizations to consider the knowledge and skills that were essential in their disciplines.

Meanwhile, the federal government was encouraging the development and implementation of educational standards. President George H. W. Bush's administration issued grants to subject-matter organizations and researchers to develop standards in a wide range of content areas, including history, English language arts, science, geography, foreign languages, the fine arts, and civics. And the Clinton administration funded states to develop their individual standards and, at least initially, authorized the creation of a federal agency that would compare state standards to the national standards. The 1994 reauthorization of the Elementary and Secondary Education Act, which President Clinton signed in October of that year, required states to adopt standards for student performance and, significantly, required these standards to be the same for all students, regardless of their economic or educational background. By the end of the decade, every state except Iowa had adopted standards in core subjects.

While some policy makers had expressed hope for the development of national standards, so that the expectations for student learning would be consistent from state to state, political divisions soon dashed those aspirations. The biggest flash point emerged over standards for U.S. history, a subject that is often contentious. The Bush administration had awarded a grant to a history center at the University of California, Los Angeles, to develop standards in that subject; the day before the standards were released, Lynne V. Cheney, who as chairwoman of the National Endowment for the Humanities had issued the grant, denounced them in an article published in the *Wall*

Street Journal, claiming that the standards had underemphasized positive stories in American history while overemphasizing the dark side. The U.S. Senate echoed her criticisms, voting 99–1 to denounce the standards.

In addition, the Clinton administration's proposal for a federal agency to oversee the development of state standards also drew attacks in Congress from critics who charged that the agency represented a "national school board," and the agency was killed before any members were appointed. Clinton's proposal to create a voluntary national test in fourth-grade reading and eighth-grade mathematics also died in Congress, because of concerns over local control over education. The idea of national standards appeared dead, and the No Child Left Behind Act, signed into law in 2002, reinforced that belief with its requirement that states set their own standards and their own definitions of what constitutes "proficiency."

The Reemergence of National Standards

Despite that view, the idea that national standards are necessary continued to thrive. Indeed, the clamor for national standards grew stronger during the first decade of the twenty-first century. There were several reasons for the renewed interest in the notion.

First, No Child Left Behind brought to the surface the wide variations in state standards. Under that law, each state was required to administer NAEP, a federally sponsored test, and reports quickly emerged that showed a wide divergence in some states in the proportion of students who were proficient on state tests, compared to the proportion of students proficient on NAEP. For example, in Tennessee in 2005, 87 percent of fourth graders were proficient on the state test in mathematics, compared with 28 percent who were proficient on NAEP. In Massachusetts, on the other hand, 40 percent of fourth graders were proficient on the state test in mathematics in 2005, compared with 41 percent on NAEP. Although there are several explanations for these discrepancies, they suggested to many policy makers that some states appeared to have lower expectations for students than others.

Second, there was a growing concern that too many students were ill-prepared for postsecondary education. About a third of all students who entered higher education were required to take at least one remedial course, and the evidence showed that students who took remedial courses were less likely to complete college than those who did not. And anecdotal reports from college professors and employers suggested that there were significant skills gaps among students who completed high school. The standards in at least some states were not high enough to prepare students for education beyond high school, policy makers concluded.

And third, evidence from international studies showed that U.S. students were not performing as well as students from other countries that were emerging as economic competitors. And the globalization of the economy meant that students graduating from high school in Alabama and Oregon were competing against students from India and China. The differences among states seemed to matter less; all standards needed to be higher to meet the worldwide competition.

Faced with these trends, policy organizations began to produce reports in the mid-2000s calling for national standards that would be higher than many state standards and that would compare favorably with those from high-performing nations. At the same time, representatives of these organizations began meeting to figure out a way to create national standards that would avoid the political pitfalls that seemed to doom the movement the decade before. One of the leaders of the effort was former governor James B. Hunt Jr. of North Carolina, who held the first meeting on the topic in the summer of 2006 in North Carolina. That meeting was followed by a larger gathering in Washington, convened by former governor Bob Wise of West Virginia.

Participants in the meetings favored national standards, but they agreed that the standards could not be developed at the national level and imposed on the states. Rather, they agreed, the best strategy was for the states to develop them collectively. Several states had already been moving in this direction. Under the auspices of Achieve, a Washington-based organization led by governors and business leaders, some three dozen states, in what was known as the American Diploma Project, had worked to align their end-of-high-school standards with the expectations of higher education and employers. The states, moreover, agreed on a common set of high school exit benchmarks in English language arts and mathematics.

On a smaller scale, the states of New Hampshire, Rhode Island, and Vermont (later joined by Maine) developed common standards and a common test. Under No Child Left Behind, these states had to expand their testing programs to include students in additional grades, and leaders in all of them recognized that they could develop a better measure of student performance if they pooled their resources. The resulting test, known as the New England Common Assessment Program (NECAP), was highly regarded.

After some deliberation, the National Governors Association (NGA) and the Council of Chief State School Officers (CCSSO) agreed to lead the effort to create common standards. The two organizations had collaborated with Achieve on a report that argued for national standards benchmarked against international standards, and the new leader of the CCSSO, Gene Wilhoit, a former state commissioner of education in Kentucky, had been an active leader in the America Diploma Project. As organizations of state leaders, the NGA and CCSSO could ensure that the initiative was state-led.

To ensure state buy-in, the NGA and CCSSO drafted a memorandum of agreement that participating states would sign to signal their commitment to participate in the project. The groups presented the memorandum at a meeting in April 2009 at an airport hotel in Chicago. It stated that participating states would agree to take part in the development of standards, but would not necessarily commit to adopting them. Governors and chief state school officers (and in some cases chairs of state boards of education) would have to sign the agreement to show support. In the end, forty-eight governors and state chiefs signed the memorandum.

Writing the Standards

The organizations involved in the common standards initiative wanted to conduct the process differently from the way most states had developed their standards. In many cases, states had gathered together a broad group of constituents, each of whom had pet ideas they wanted to include in the standards. In an effort to get widespread buy-in, the standards committees accepted all of the ideas, resulting in long lists of topics—far more than any teacher could address in a school year. In addition, the states tended to write each grade level set of standards independently, meaning that there was often little coherence from grade to grade. As one study found, students were more likely to encounter the same topic when they moved from, say, fourth grade to fifth grade in the same state than they would if they moved during a year to a different state.

By contrast, the Common Core Standards initiative leaders had a different point of view. They were influenced strongly by a report written by two young scholars, David Coleman and Jason Zimba, who had criticized the standards states had developed as unhelpful to students and teachers. Their report, entitled "Math and Science Standards That Are Fewer, Clearer, Higher to Raise Achievement at All Levels," argued for a more parsimonious set of standards that would guide instruction.[3] "Fewer, clearer, higher" became the mantra of the Common Core State Standards effort, and Coleman and Zimba became lead authors of the Standards—Coleman in English language arts and Zimba in mathematics. After the Standards were released, they formed an organization called Student Achievement Partners, which provides support to teachers in implementing them (Coleman is now the president of the College Board).

To adhere to those principles, the initiative's leaders adopted a set of criteria for the standards writers. The first criterion was that the Common Core Standards should address college and career readiness. That is, the Standards should identify the knowledge and skills that were essential for students' postsecondary success; any topics that were not required for that goal would be dropped. The initiative leaders insisted that the writers rely on evidence of college and career readiness; however, the evidence did not have to be airtight. The best available research would do.

A second key criterion was international benchmarking. Because of the interest among policy makers in international competitiveness, the initiative leaders wanted to ensure that the Standards were comparable to those of the best-performing nations.

To write the Standards, the organizations leading the effort agreed to divide the work into two parts. First, they would set standards for the end of high school that would indicate college and career readiness. These standards would represent the end point of a student's school career; the standards for early grades would lead to those ends. To draw up this first set of standards, the leaders enlisted researchers and practitioners associated with Achieve, ACT, and the College Board, organizations with expertise in the expectations for higher education and the workplace.

The group conducted research into the requirements for first-year college courses and workplace training programs—including poring through entry-level course textbooks—and drafted a set of standards for all students. The group vetted them with a "feedback group" of leading experts, after which they submitted the standards for public comment. Nearly a thousand educators, parents, and students offered comments, and the group then revised them again.

Meanwhile, the initiative leaders set up a separate group to write the grade-by-grade standards that were intended to lead to the standards for college and career readiness. Because of the intricacies involved in this process, the leaders broadened the writing group to include individuals with expertise in assessment, curriculum design, cognitive development, and English language acquisition. As before, the leaders also established feedback groups of experts to review drafts in advance of public comment. The leaders also established a "validation committee," composed of leading researchers, teachers, and administrators, to pass judgment on whether the product reflected research on college and career readiness and the expectations of high-performing nations.

After months of discussion, the writing teams released a draft of grade-by-grade standards for public comment. This time, some ten thousand people commented, some with general ideas, some with more specific suggestions. The writing teams weighed these remarks, revised their drafts, and released a final version. The validation committee reported that the final version indeed met the initiative's criteria. The standards were released to the public at a ceremony in Suwanee, Georgia, on June 2, 2010.

The Race to Adopt

Kentucky did not wait for the final version of the Common Core Standards to be released before state officials agreed to adopt them. Under legislation passed the previous year by the state legislature, the state had set in motion a process for approving new standards for student performance and implementing them through new curriculum and teacher-education standards. The state board of education adopted the Common Core in February (subject to review of the final version), and asked the boards that oversee higher education and teacher preparation to incorporate the Standards into postsecondary coursework and requirements for prospective teachers.

Since then, Kentucky has gone much further to implement the Common Core State Standards. For example, the Kentucky Department of Education prepared an extensive analysis that compared the Common Core with Kentucky's previous standards, and distributed it widely. Kentucky Educational Television also prepared online modules for parents, teachers, and community members to explain the Standards, and the Pritchard Committee, a statewide organization of civic leaders, developed a campaign to explain the Standards and why they matter to parents and community members across the state.

The education department also built an online technology platform, known as Kentucky's Continuous Instructional Improvement Technology System, that will make available lessons, tests, and curriculum materials at the click of a mouse. The system will also include podcasts produced by higher education faculty to help educate teachers about new instructional strategies designed around the standards.

Three other states—Hawaii, Maryland, and West Virginia—adopted the Standards conditionally prior to their formal release. Then, once they were released, dozens of state boards of education added their votes. Twenty-seven states adopted the Standards by the end of July; by the end of 2010, forty-three states and the District of Columbia had done so. Two more states adopted them in 2011, and in 2012, the school district of Anchorage, Alaska, one of the few states that had not adopted the standards, adopted them on their own, as did the Department of Defense Education Activity. By the end of 2012, the Common Core State Standards were the standards for forty-six states, the District of Columbia, and the Department of Defense schools.[4]

Why did nearly every state agree to accept these standards? In part, they had an incentive to do so. In 2009 the U.S. Department of Education launched the Race to the Top program, which provided up to $4.3 billion in grants to states that pursued a set of reforms that included upgrading standards. The program gave additional points to states that adopted the Common Core State Standards by August 2, 2010; however, contrary to a widely held myth, the department did not require states to adopt the Common Core Standards in order to win Race to the Top grants. A survey of state officials by the Center for Education Policy found that the federal incentive helped, but the quality of the Standards themselves was the most important factor in their adoption decision. In at least two states, the federal connection proved a disincentive to adoption.[5]

According to testimony from state officials, state boards agreed to adopt the Common Core State Standards because they believed that their existing standards were inadequate and that the Common Core would accelerate educational improvement. In most cases the votes for adoption were unanimous. However, in a few cases, the debate was contentious. Take Massachusetts, for example. There, the state's standards were highly regarded and were considered an important factor in the state's high level of academic performance on NAEP. Advocates of the existing standards produced a report that concluded that the Massachusetts standards were superior to the Common Core; Common Core advocates commissioned a separate study that came to the opposite conclusion. In the end, the education board voted to adopt the Common Core Standards.

Similarly, in California, a state with equally highly regarded standards (though lower levels of student performance), supporters of the state's mathematics standards resisted the Common Core and insisted on changes. Under the rules governing the adoption process, states could add to the Standards but could not delete any; the idea was to ensure that they remain common and coherent across states. The California Board of Education added some standards to the middle grades to ensure that students would be prepared to take algebra in eighth grade. With those revisions, the state board adopted the Common Core Standards.

In a few states, there have been attempts to rescind or at least reconsider the adoption of the Common Core. In Alabama, for example, the state board, which had undergone a change in personnel after the 2010 election, reconsidered its adoption decision, but voted to uphold it, despite the opposition of the newly elected governor. In other states, such as South Carolina, legislators proposed measures to give the legislature a say in adoption, but none of those measures passed. The Common Core Standards remain the standards in nearly every state.

What's Next?

Adopting standards is only the first step in educational improvement. The goal is for students to meet the standards, and for that to happen, the standards need to be implemented in every classroom. That means that states, districts, schools, and private organizations need to develop assessments that measure performance against the standards, to create and adopt curriculum materials aligned to the standards, and to put in place professional development to ensure that teachers are capable of teaching what the standards expect.

Since the release of the Common Core Standards there has been an extraordinary outpouring of activity to implement them. To be sure, these efforts are uneven, and the quality is uncertain. Whether they will reach their goal remains to be seen. But the effort far exceeds the implementation of state standards in the 1990s and early 2000s.

The most extensive implementation undertaking is the development of assessments to measure performance against the Standards. In 2010 the U.S. Department of Education awarded a total of $330 million to two consortia of states that had proposed to create assessments of the Common Core Standards. The two consortia—the Partnership for Assessment of Readiness for College and Careers (PARCC), consisting of twenty-two states, and the Smarter Balanced Assessment Consortium (SBAC), consisting of twenty-four states (one is currently a member of both consortia)—have committed to putting new assessments in place by the 2014–2015 school year.[6]

The two consortia have laid out ambitious plans for these new assessments. Both plan to administer them on computers, and both plan to use extended performance tasks that ask students to conduct research, write extensively, and undertake complex mathematical problems. The consortia also plan to provide resources for teachers to use throughout the school year. There are many logistical, technical, and political issues that need to be resolved before these assessments are put in place, and the final shape of the assessments remains to be seen. But if the consortia remain true to their vision, these assessments will go a long way toward advancing the implementation of the Common Core Standards in classrooms.

In addition to the assessments, there is tremendous activity under way to develop new curriculum materials aligned to the Standards. Commercial publishers, seeing for the first time a near-national market, are creating textbooks and other materials to support classroom instruction around the Common Core. Many of these use technology in new ways; for example, Pearson, a major publishing firm, is developing a K–12 series of curriculum materials designed to align with the Common Core Standards. The materials, developed with input from members of the teams that wrote the Standards, will be delivered completely online, through tablets like the iPad. They will include projects for students to complete, texts and digital materials to support students in conducting their projects, and assessments to check student understanding. The firm has received support for this effort from the Bill and Melinda Gates Foundation; as a condition of this support, some of the materials will be available to all schools free of charge.

To create incentives for other publishers to do the same, the Council of Great City Schools, an organization representing large urban school districts, has agreed to use its collective purchasing power to persuade publishers to produce materials that are aligned with the Common Core Standards. The council's districts have adopted a set of criteria they will use to evaluate curriculum materials for alignment.

There are also unprecedented efforts to prepare teachers to understand the Standards and help them revise their instruction around them. As noted above, Kentucky has developed a Web-based portal with lesson plans and related materials; other states are developing similar platforms. And private organizations, such as Student Achievement Partners, a New York City–based organization led by some of the lead writers of the Common Core Standards, are also holding workshops for teachers and sharing lesson plans and other materials.

Teacher education institutions are also revamping their programs to help ensure that new teachers are prepared to teach to the Common Core Standards. For example, a group of mathematics educators, known as the Mathematics Teacher Education Partnership, has launched an effort to work with middle and high school teachers to revamp teacher preparation programs to ensure that new teachers are prepared to teach to the expectations of the Common Core. The partnership is lining up potential participants; the initial planning committee includes educators from eight states.

The Road Ahead

Whether all of these efforts will be effective—and if effective, be sufficient to transform teaching and learning in nearly every classroom—will be the major test of the next few years. There are many challenges that stand in the way.

For example, although the assessments are intended to be administered on computers, many districts lack the hardware and bandwidth necessary to undertake online assessments. Districts and states will need to upgrade their technology or find ways to accommodate the new assessments. In addition, states will have to wrestle with the fact that these new assessments will likely show that student performance appears lower than it has over the past decade. Because many states have used tests that measured relatively low-level knowledge and skills, students may be unaccustomed to assessments that ask them to write extensively or solve complex problems. States and schools need to be able to reassure the public that these results are a more realistic assessment of their students' abilities, and that they are putting in place support for teachers and students so that test scores will rise in the coming years.

The good news is that teachers and parents strongly support the Common Core Standards. Polls have shown that people believe the Standards are a positive step that can improve teaching and learning, and that they will lead to a greater consistency in education across states.

But the first step toward ensuring that the Standards can help schools reach this goal is an understanding of what the Standards actually suggest for classroom instruction. That is what the remainder of this book aims to describe.

CHAPTER

2

Less Is More

FOCUS, FOCUS, FOCUS

The results of the Third International Mathematics and Science Study (TIMSS), released in 1996, attracted a great deal of headlines and attention with its finding that U.S. students performed well below the level of their peers from other countries. Although fourth graders performed relatively well—in science, the fourth graders were among the best in the world—eighth graders performed just below the international average in mathematics, and twelfth graders were at the bottom of the international rankings, outperforming only students from Cyprus and South Africa.

Other cross-national assessments had previously shown that U.S. students performed less well than those of other countries, particularly in mathematics, but TIMSS (now known as Trends in International Mathematics and Science Study) was the best-designed study of its kind, measuring achievement in forty-two nations. The results appeared at a time when Americans were increasingly aware of globalization and concerned about the nation's standing in the world economy. And subsequent international assessments, including later versions of TIMSS as well as the Programme for International Student Assessment (PISA), a test administered to fifteen-year-olds, confirmed the relative poor showing of U.S. students.

Yet while the "horse race" drew the most attention, some of the most interesting findings from TIMSS were those that examined possible explanations for the differences in performance among the participating countries. And the results pointed to a clear conclusion: U.S. performance lagged because the United States lacked a clear, coherent curriculum. In a phrase that became famous, William Schmidt and his fellow researchers concluded that the U.S. mathematics curriculum was "a mile wide and an inch deep."

The researchers reached this conclusion by examining state standards and the textbooks that have been produced to follow them. They found that the U.S. standards and materials include far more topics than other countries do, and that their coverage of these topics is relatively superficial, with long lists of unrelated topics being repeated year after year. By eighth grade, the researchers found, U.S. mathematics textbooks include about thirty topics—everything from common fractions, polygons, and circles to proportionality problems and two-dimensional coordinate geometry—which is three times the number found in Japanese textbooks.

As Schmidt and his colleagues explain, these findings have implications for how mathematics is taught and learned:

> As a result of these poorly designed standards and textbooks, the curriculum that is enacted in the U.S. (compared to the rest of the world) is highly repetitive, unfocused, unchallenging, and incoherent, especially during the middle-school years. There is an important implication here. Our teachers work in a context that demands that they teach a lot of things, but nothing in-depth. We truly have standards, and thus enacted curricula, that are a "mile wide and an inch deep."
>
> One popular response to a study like TIMSS is to blame the teachers. But the teachers in our country are simply doing what we have asked them to do: "Teach everything you can. Don't worry about depth. Your goal is to teach 35 things briefly, not 10 things well."[1]

Looking more deeply, Schmidt and his colleagues found that the lack of focus in mathematic standards affected student learning—not only in the United States, but across all countries that participated in TIMSS. They found that greater coverage within the curriculum for a particular topic, with more demanding expectations, related to higher mathematics achievement. That is, countries whose standards included fewer topics, taught in greater depth, performed better than countries with a "mile-wide, inch-deep" problem.[2]

Following the release of the TIMSS results, Achieve, a Washington-based organization led by governors and business leaders, asked Schmidt to conduct a more detailed examination of twenty-one state standards, using the TIMSS methodology. His analysis confirmed his previous findings: U.S. state standards included far more topics than other countries' standards do. The problem is particularly acute in middle school, he found, because topics tend to remain in standards year after year, whereas other countries appear to expect students to master topics and move on. For example, Oregon's standards for grades three, five, eight, and ten repeated the expectation that students would be able to round numbers (to the nearest 10, 100, and 1,000 in grade three; and to the nearest 1,000 and nearest 1,000,000 in grade eight). Japan, by contrast, expected students to understand the place value of 10,000 in grade three and to understand units as large as billion in grade four.[3]

David Coleman and Jason Zimba, the young scholars who called for "fewer, clearer, higher" standards in a 2007 paper that proved enormously influential for the Common Core State Standards (see chapter 1), also found that the large number of topics in state standards impeded learning and achievement. Coleman and Zimba had started an organization called the Grow Network, which attempted to provide support to teachers to use state test results to improve instruction. However, they found that teachers' tasks were exceedingly difficult, because the extensive standards meant that they were expected to cover so much material. "The current system prevents *most* students from mastering *anything at all,*" they wrote. "Even if they reach the proficient level in every standard, they will be a long way from mastery of any of them—with no realistic way to get there, because of the insistence on covering everything."[4]

Coleman and Zimba called for standards that are "fewer, clearer, higher," and laid out a set of "filters" for states to use to boil down standards to the most essential. This argument became extremely influential. The organizers of the Common Core State Standards used it to set out criteria for the standards, and "fewer, clearer, higher" became the mantra of the Standards effort (as well as the title of this book). Both Coleman and Zimba went on to take leading roles in the standards-development process—Coleman in English language arts and Zimba in mathematics, and they continued to exert influence in providing assistance to teachers in implementing the Standards.

What Focus Looks Like

To get an idea of what a focused set of mathematics standards looks like, consider Japan's. As noted above, Japanese standards include far fewer topics than American state standards tended to include, and Japan performed among the highest of all countries on TIMSS.

Figure 2.1 shows Japan's standards for grade one, and figure 2.2 for grade eight:

FIGURE 2.1

Japan's mathematics standards
Grade 1

A. Numbers and Calculations
   (1) Through activities such as counting the numbers of concrete objects, to help pupils understand the meaning of numbers and use numbers.
      a. To compare numbers of objects by making one-to-one correspondence between objects.
      b. To correctly count or represent the number and order of objects.
      c. To make a sequence of numbers and to put numbers on a number line by judging the size and the order of the numbers.
      d. To consider a number in relation to other numbers by regarding it as a sum or difference of other numbers.
      e. To understand the representations of two-digit numbers.

f. To get to know the representations of three-digit numbers in simple cases.
g. To consider numbers using ten as a unit.

(2) To help pupils understand the meaning of addition and subtraction and use the calculations.
a. To get to know situations where addition and subtraction are used.
b. To explore ways of addition of two one-digit numbers, and subtraction as the inverse operation, and to do these calculations accurately.
c. To explore ways of addition and subtraction of two-digit numbers and so on in simple cases.

B. Quantities and Measurements

(1) Through activities such as comparing sizes of concrete objects, to help pupils enrich their experiences that will form the foundation for understanding quantities and measurements.
a. To directly compare length, area, and volume.
b. To compare quantities by using familiar objects as a unit in terms of multiples of it.

(2) To help pupils read clock times in their daily lives.

C. Geometrical Figures

(1) Through activities such as observing and composing the shapes of familiar objects, to help pupils enrich their experiences that will form the foundation for understanding geometrical figures.
a. To recognize the shapes of objects, and to grasp their features.
b. To express the position of an object by correctly using the words concerning direction and position such as "front and rear," "right and left," and "above and below."

D. Mathematical Relations

(1) To help pupils represent situations where addition and subtraction are used, by using algebraic expressions, and interpret these expressions.

(2) To help pupils represent the number of objects using pictures or figures, and interpret them.

Source: Ministry of Education, Sports, Culture, and Science, Japan.

FIGURE 2.2

Japan's mathematics standards

Grade 8

A. Numbers and Algebraic Expressions

(1) To foster the ability to find out relationships of numbers and quantities in concrete phenomena, represent these relationships in algebraic expressions using letters, and read the meaning of these expressions, and to be able to calculate the four fundamental operations with expressions using letters.

a. To calculate addition and subtraction with simple polynomials, as well as multiplication and division with monomials.

b. To understand how to grasp and explain numbers and quantities and the relationships of numbers and quantities in algebraic expressions using letters.

c. To transform simple algebraic expressions according to the purpose.

(2) To understand simultaneous linear equations with two unknowns, and to be able to consider by using it.

a. To understand the meaning of linear equations with two unknowns and their solutions.

b. To understand the necessity and meaning of simultaneous linear equations with two unknowns and the meaning of their solutions.

c. To solve simple simultaneous linear equations with two unknowns and make use of them in concrete situations.

Terms and Symbols

similar term

B. Geometrical Figures

(1) Through activities like observation, manipulation, and experimentation, to be able to find out the properties of basic plane figures and verify them based on the properties of parallel lines.

a. To understand the properties of parallel lines and angles and basing on it, to verify and explain the properties of geometrical figures.

b. To know how to find out the properties of angles of polygons based on the properties of parallel lines and angles of triangle.

(2) To understand the congruence of geometrical figures and deepen the way of viewing geometrical figures, to verify the properties of geometrical figures based on the facts like the conditions for congruence of triangles, and to foster the ability to think and represent logically.

a. To understand the meaning of congruence of plane figures and the conditions for congruence of triangles.

b. To understand the necessity, meaning, and methods of proof.

c. To logically verify the basic properties of triangles and parallelograms based on the facts like the conditions for congruence of triangles, and to find out new properties by reading proofs of the properties of geometrical figures.

Terms and Symbols

opposite angle, interior angle, exterior angle, definition, proof, converse

C. Functions

(1) Through finding out two numbers/quantities in concrete phenomena and exploring their change and correspondence, to understand linear functions, and to foster the ability to find out, represent, and think about functional relationships.

a. To know that in concrete phenomena there are some phenomena which can be grasped as linear functions.

b. To understand linear functions by interrelating their tables, algebraic expressions, and graphs.

c. To recognize linear equations with two unknowns as algebraic expressions representing functions.

d. To grasp and explain concrete phenomena by using linear functions.

Source: Ministry of Education, Sports, Culture, and Science, Japan.

As these examples indicate, Japan's standards are extraordinarily lean. The first-grade standards include just four topics: numbers and calculations, quantities and measurements, geometrical figures, and mathematical relations. And the eighth-grade standards include just three: numbers and algebraic expressions, geometrical figures, and functions. This means that teachers in these two grades spend their time concentrating on those topics, and exploring them in depth so that students understand them. It also means that teachers do not spend time on other topics that might be taught in other grades, or that are less relevant for student understanding.

One reason the Japanese standards are able to maintain their focus is that they do not include the same topic from year to year, as many American state standards have tended to do. Japan expects students to master topics and move on, not to pile up standards like geological strata.

While Japan's standards are considered exemplary, they are not unique. Other countries that perform well on international mathematics assessments, such as the Czech and Slovak Republics and South Korea, also have relatively parsimonious and focused standards for mathematics education. Conversely, New Zealand and the United States, both of which performed below the international average on TIMSS, include the most topics in their eighth-grade standards.

How to Achieve Focus

William McCallum, a professor of mathematics at the University of Arizona and a lead writer of the Common Core mathematics standards, has said that countries like Japan, which have a national ministry of education, are better able to develop focused standards than the United States, where responsibility for education is more diffuse.[5] But the Common Core Standards initiative has provided an opportunity to wipe the slate clean and consider what standards should be included.

In their influential 2007 paper, Coleman and Zimba outlined the filters, or criteria, that should be used to determine whether a particular topic should be included in a set of standards. These are:

1. Is it mathematically important, both for further study in mathematics and for use in applications in and outside of school?
2. Does it "fit" with what is known about learning mathematics?
3. Does it connect logically with the mathematics in earlier and later grade levels?
4. Can it wait until later grades? And should it?
5. Can it be started earlier, and is there a benefit in starting earlier?
6. Is it truly necessary for college and work and thus should be provided for all, or an element of advanced math for only some students to pursue?
7. Is this content most effectively learned years in advance of its use, or closer to the actual moment of application in work or college?[6]

The first three are from the National Council of Teachers of Mathematics document known as Focal Points, which was developed to identify the most critical of the standards developed by the organization. But Coleman and Zimba argued that standards writers, and thus states, needed additional criteria to ensure that standards are indeed the most essential for all students to learn. As they put it, "Our burden of proof needs to shift so that each piece of content earns its way in."[7]

Following through on that principle proved challenging, according to Zimba. In a 2013 interview, he recalled that the standards writers faced constant pressure from educators lobbying for their favorite topics. "People kept saying, 'We love the focus of these standards! Now if you could just add this one thing . . .' It wasn't easy for the writers to hold the line. We couldn't have done it without a uniquely designed development process—one that privileged evidence and argument."[8]

What pieces of content earned their way in to the Common Core Standards? The focus in the Standards is immediately evident in the standards for the elementary grades. At first glance, it may appear as though the elementary standards are nearly as numerous as those of the state standards they were intended to replace. For example, in kindergarten, there are five "domains," which are the counterparts to the "topics" in Schmidt's study:

counting and cardinality, operations and algebraic thinking, number and operations in Base 10, measurement and data, and geometry. And there are from one to three standards in each domain. But a closer look shows that four of the five domains are about number and operations. The same is true in every grade through grade five. Thus, like the Japanese standards, the Common Core State Standards in mathematics focus intensively in the early grades on just two big topics—number and geometry.

What is missing to achieve this focus? One of the most obvious omissions is the area of data, which is "reduced to a trickle," according to McCallum:

> This was one of the more controversial shifts in the Common Core . . . Debate about curriculum in the United States has suffered from an all-or-nothing quality, and nowhere is this seen more clearly than in the debate about data and statistics in elementary school: it has seemed that the only choices were embracing a rich stream on data work in elementary school . . . or drying it up to nothing. In contrast, the Common Core is based on progressions that start with a trickle before they grow into the full flow of a domain. Thus the data standards in elementary school are neither to be ignored nor to be given undue prominence. In due time, in high school, statistics and probability becomes a major topic.[9]

That is not to say that data is absent from the elementary standards. But in general, the data standards are in service to the main instructional focus: number and geometry. For instance, in third grade, a standard under "represent and interpret data" states: "Draw a scaled picture graph and a scaled bar graph to represent a data set with several categories" (3.MD.3). As an example, it continues, students can draw a bar graph in which each square in the bar graph represents five pets. In that way, the data standard helps support the third-grade focus on multiplication.

Likewise, functions—usually expressed as "patterns" in elementary school—are also reduced to a trickle in the Common Core, with standards in grades three, four, and five intended to prepare students for the full study of functions in middle school. For instance, in grade four, students are expected to be able to "generate a number or shape pattern that follows a given rule" (4.OA.5). As an example, students, given the rule "add 3" and starting with 1, would be expected to show how the sequence proceeds and to observe that the numbers in the pattern alternate between odd and even. They then would be expected to explain informally why the numbers would continue to alternate this way. Thus this standard prepares students for a subsequent study of $y = x + 3$.

The emphasis on a focused set of topics continues in the middle school standards. In sixth grade the major areas of focus include ratios and proportional reasoning, the number system, and expressions and equations. Statistics and probability and geometry are also included in the sixth-grade standards, but most of the standards at that grade focus on other topics. By eighth grade, the major areas of emphasis are expressions and equations, functions, and geometry.

"Teach Less, Learn More"

The goal of focus in the mathematics standards is, as a Singapore education slogan put it, "Teach Less, Learn More." By reducing the number of topics teachers are expected to cover, the standards enable teachers to slow down their teaching so that students can explore concepts in greater depth and learn them more effectively.

Vibha Mahadeo, a mathematics teacher at IS 187 in New York City, saw firsthand how that could work. Her school began to implement the Common Core Standards in seventh grade, but her eighth-grade classes continued to use the state standards. "In my 8th class, for instance, I teach everything from pre-algebra, to geometry, graphing parabolas, trigonometry. Things that they don't even understand why. And I don't have the time," she said on a Teaching Channel video. "So I enjoy that the Common Core Standards has cut down on a lot of that and picked a few things that we can really understand."

For example, in a unit on dilations, a geometric concept that enables the creation of scale drawings, Mahadeo had students try their own methods for figuring out solutions, rather than telling them the solution, which would be faster. By slowing the classroom down, Mahadeo made sure that the students justified their approach, which showed that they understood the concept.

Starting Points

While the Standards themselves were designed to focus on a relatively small number of topics, particular topics within the Standards are especially critical to enabling students to move on to more advanced topics. A number of resources developed to support the implementation of the Common Core State Standards have identified the topics that are most ripe for in-depth focus.

One such resource is a model content framework developed by the Partnership for Assessment of Readiness for College and Careers (PARCC), which, as described in chapter 1, is one of two state consortia developing assessments to measure student performance against the Common Core State Standards. The framework is not a curriculum; rather, it is a suggestion for how schools can design instructional programs to lead students toward attainment of the Standards.

The PARCC framework for mathematics states that teachers are unlikely to shift to all the Standards at once. To provide guidance, it offers a suggested list of key topics as "starting points" for the transition to the Common Core Standards. These topics were selected, the document states, to "define content boundaries" to help provide focus in the creation of new materials and assessments aligned to the Standards.

The "starting points" for mathematics are:

- Counting and Cardinality and Operations and Algebraic Thinking (particularly in the development of an understanding of quantity): grades K–2.
- Operations and Algebraic Thinking: multiplication and division in grades 3–5, tracing the evolving meaning of multiplication from equal groups and array/area thinking in grade 3 to all multiplication situations in grade 4 (including multiplicative comparisons) and from whole numbers in grade 3 to decimals and fractions in grades 5 and 6.
- Number and Operations in Base Ten: addition and subtraction in grades 1–4.

- Number and Operations in Base Ten: multiplication and division in grades 3–6.
- Number and Operations – Fractions: fraction addition and subtraction in grades 4–5, including related development of fraction equivalence in grades 3–5.
- Number and Operations – Fractions: fraction multiplication and division in grades 4–6.
- The Number System: grades 6–7.
- Expressions and Equations: grades 6–8, including how this extends prior work in arithmetic.
- Ratio and Proportional Reasoning: its development in grades 6–7, its relationship to functional thinking in grades 6–8, and its connection to lines and linear equations in grade 8.
- Geometry: work with the coordinate plane in grades 5–8, including connections to ratio, proportion, algebra, and functions in grades 6–high school.
- Geometry: congruence and similarity of figures in grades 8–high school, with emphasis on real-world and mathematical problems involving scales and connections to ratio and proportion.
- Modeling: focused on equations and inequalities in high school, development from simple modeling tasks such as word problems to richer, more open-ended modeling tasks.
- Seeing Structure in Expressions: from expressions appropriate to grades 8–9 to expressions appropriate to grades 10–11.
- Statistics and Probability: comparing populations and drawing inferences in grades 6–high school.
- Units as a Cross-cutting Theme: in the areas of measurement, geometric measurement, base-ten arithmetic, unit fractions, and fraction arithmetic, including the role of the number line.[10]

The document also recommends subsets of the Standards for each grade that present opportunities for in-depth focus. For example, in grade four, the document suggests focusing on a standard for fractions: "extend understanding of fraction equivalence and ordering" (4.NF.1). That standard is important, the document states, because "extending fraction equivalence to the general case is necessary to extend arithmetic from whole numbers to fractions and decimals."[11] Similarly, the document also suggests a focus on the standard for building fractions from unit fractions. That standard is an important step on the multigrade progression of learning to add, subtract, multiply, and divide fractions, the framework document states.

The more intensive focus, this document suggests, can turn a "mile-wide, inch-deep" curriculum into one that is relatively narrow but a mile deep.

CHAPTER

3

Achieving Coherence

One of the most important findings from cognitive science over the past few years has been the notion that experts in a particular area, like mathematics, differ from novices in significant ways. Not only do they know more about the subject; they also approach problems differently and organize their knowledge more effectively to help solve them.

To take one often-cited example, studies of chess players found that experts are much better able than novices to remember the placement of chess pieces on a board when they are arranged in a meaningful formation. That is because expert players can see and recognize patterns that novices cannot.[1]

Armed with that knowledge, researchers have been mapping the pathways from the novice state to expertise in an effort to identify the steps learners take to become more proficient in a subject area. These pathways, often called learning progressions, have been developed in many subject areas, particularly in mathematics and science, and have informed the development of curriculum and assessments.

The Common Core State Standards in mathematics are intended to map out learning progressions in each domain of the subject to enable young people to progress, grade to grade, from rudimentary skills to college and career readiness. The Standards aim to draw a coherent pathway that will enable learning to build on prior knowledge; by contrast, many previous state standards tended to repeat topics year after year.

At the same time, the Standards deliberately strive for coherence within grades. That is, the Standards link topics with similar properties, such as statistics and algebra, so that they make more sense to teachers and to students.

The shift toward greater coherence will require some adjustments for teachers who have been accustomed to teaching the same topics in the same ways. But it might make it easier for them to know what students coming into their classrooms were expected to learn the previous years and what they will be expected to learn in subsequent years.

Learning Progressions

A recent paper on learning progressions in mathematics, or as the authors refer to them, learning trajectories, suggests that the idea might seem obvious, but its implications are profound:

> All conceptions of trajectories or progressions have roots in the unsurprising observation that the amount and complexity of students' knowledge and skill in any domain starts out small and, with effective instruction, becomes much larger over time, and that the amount of growth clearly varies with experience and instruction but also seems to reflect factors associated with maturation, as well as significant individual differences in abilities, dispositions, and interests. Trajectories or progressions are ways of characterizing what happens in between any given set of beginning and endpoints and, in an educational context, describe what seems to be involved in helping students get to particular desired endpoints.[2]

Mathematics instruction has long been built on this idea. Textbooks, for example, have been designed to present a "scope and sequence" approach that helps teachers lead students along the path toward greater knowledge and understanding. In recent decades, however, researchers have attempted to document the specific progressions students take toward greater levels of mastery. The difference between this approach and previous scope-and-sequence descriptions is that the more recent approaches are empirically based; that is, they use evidence of students' actual learning to show the particular steps along the way toward expertise and the particular instructional experiences that might support such learning.

Although the research is fairly new, it has shown some results. For example, researchers have demonstrated the growth of children's understanding of linear measurement: from measuring by laying units end to end, to measuring units by repeating a unit (e.g., one inch, two inches, three inches, and so forth), to measuring consistently, using partial units (e.g., eight half-inches).[3] However, researchers caution that the progressions that they have mapped out are neither natural nor inevitable. Some children might develop at a different rate or along a different pathway, depending on their instructional experiences and other factors. But the progressions suggest the most likely pathway and way stations.

Implications for Instruction

The notion of learning progressions clearly has important implications for instruction. By examining the expected progressions, teachers can assess where students are on the trajectories and tailor their instruction to keep them on track.

For example, teachers from a project in Vermont gave fifth-grade students a set of word problems in whole-number multiplication. One student got 80 percent of the problems right. In many cases, teachers would view that result as a sign that the student was able to move on to more advanced concepts. However, when examining the student's responses, the teacher saw that he had used repeated addition to arrive at the answers. But because the teacher had learned about learning progressions from the National Research Council and other sources, she knew that the student lacked a grasp of the concept of multiplication and was thus unable to begin multiplication of decimals or solve problems involving proportionality. She was able to identify the student's mistaken strategy and address it directly.

Some of the most important implications of the idea involve assessment. By building assessments according to learning progressions, schools and school systems could provide information on where precisely a student's performance falls along the progression. That information would be extremely valuable to teachers and would be much more useful than the information provided by any current tests, which generally indicate the performance of students relative to other students.

Some of the pioneering work in using learning progressions as a basis for assessment has taken place in Australia. Australia's Developmental Assessment program, for example, is based on "progress maps" that can track students' progress in learning over time. They indicate that, in mathematics, students in first grade can be expected to count collections of objects to show how many there are; students in second grade are expected to count forward and backward from any whole number; students in third grade are expected to count in common fractional amounts; students in fourth grade are expected to count in decimal fraction amounts; and students in fifth grade are expected to use common equivalences between decimals, fractions, and percentages. Thus students, parents, and teachers can see from the results whether students are demonstrating increased skill from one grade to the next.

As an influential National Research Council report stated, identifying these learning progressions can be difficult, but it can be done through research on how children learn. "There is no single way in which knowledge is represented by competent performers, and there is no single path to competence," the report states. "But some paths are traveled more than others. When large samples of learners are studied, a few predominant patterns tend to emerge."[4]

Implications for Standards

If education systems are intended to build students' competence in core subjects and prepare them for the future, one might think that standards for student learning would spell out the progression of learning students should follow throughout their school career. Too often, though, state standards have failed to do so. In fact, a study by Andrew Porter and his colleagues at the University of Pennsylvania found that state standards tended to repeat the same content year after year. A student was more likely to encounter the same content moving from, say, fourth grade to fifth grade in Arizona than she would if she moved from Arizona to California in the middle of fourth grade. As Porter put it at a meeting of the National Research Council, the repetition across grades sends the message: "Don't you dare learn this the first time we teach it; otherwise you'll be bored out of your skull in the subsequent grades."[5]

Porter's study corroborated the findings of researchers who analyzed data from the Third International Mathematics and Science Study (TIMSS). As we saw in chapter 2, William Schmidt and his colleagues examined standards and textbooks from the United States and compared them to materials from other nations that participated in the study. Their analysis showed that the U.S. standards tended to lack focus and included many more topics than other countries' materials tended to include—the curriculum was "a mile wide and an inch deep." But the study also showed that, in contrast to high-performing nations, the U.S. standards and materials lacked coherence. They did not specify a path toward competence, while other countries did so.

Specifically, the study looked at the top-performing countries (which the researchers called "A+ countries") and identified topics that were common to at least two-thirds of them. The results showed a clear pattern: these countries introduced a few topics in early grades, then dropped those and introduced new topics in later grades. For example, all of the A+ countries included whole number meaning, whole number operations, and measurement units in grades one, two, and three. While most continued measurement units in grades four and five, many dropped whole numbers in those grades and added new topics, such as common fractions and decimal fractions. And in grades six through eight, these topics were dropped in turn, and topics such as proportionality, equations and formulas, and 3-D geometry were introduced.

In the United States, the patterns were not so clear. Topics introduced in first grade, like measurement units, were continued throughout the grades. And most states included topics introduced in later grades in other countries, like 3-D geometry, as early as first grade, and continued them each year.

Though the U.S. curriculum structure might appear haphazard, it actually is based on an earlier theory of how children learn. In the early 1960s Jerome Bruner, a pioneering cognitive psychologist at Harvard University, developed the idea of a "spiral" curriculum, in which students are introduced to topics early and study them in greater and greater depth over time.[6]

Thus, students could be taught a rudimentary version of 3-D geometry in the primary grades and then build on their understanding when the topic is reviewed in later grades.

In practice, though, the spiral was "wound too tight," as some critics contended. Schools spent so much time reviewing material, there was little time left for new topics. And the situation was worse for low-performing students. As Adam Gamoran, the John D. MacArthur Professor of Sociology and Educational Policy Studies at the University of Wisconsin, Madison, put it, "American students who perform poorly in arithmetic are subject to a special form of the spiral curriculum, which might be called the 'circular curriculum': they repeat arithmetic over and over until they stop studying mathematics."[7]

The experience of other countries as well as new findings in cognitive science, such as the development of learning progressions, suggested a different approach.

Learning Progressions and the Common Core State Standards

The Common Core State Standards state clearly that they were crafted with a firm grounding in learning progressions: "The development of these Standards began with research-based learning progressions detailing what is known today about how students' mathematical knowledge, skill, and understanding develop over time."[8] However, the authors acknowledge that research does not exist on all possible learning trajectories in mathematics. The Standards represent the best available hypothesis in 2010.

The structure and language of the Standards were designed to show the progressions explicitly. For example, the focus of the number and operations standards in grade one is on addition and subtraction; the focus in grade three is on multiplication and division. But the language of the standards in both grades is similar, to show that these represent a progression toward a more advanced topics. In kindergarten, a standard reads: "Solve addition and subtraction word problems, and add and subtract within 10, e.g., by using objects or drawings to represent the problem" (K.OA.2) A standard in grade three reads: "Use multiplication and division within 100 to solve word problems in situations involving equal groups, arrays, and measurement quantities, e.g., by using drawings and equations with a symbol for the unknown number to represent the problem" (3.OA.3). This represents a progression from addition and subtraction to multiplication and division, and from single digits to double digits.

Similarly, the standards show a progression in measurement by using similar language to describe expectations for the measurement of two- and three-dimensional figures. Here are the standards for area in grade three (3.MD.5–7):

Geometric measurement: understand concepts of area and relate area to multiplication and to addition.

5. Recognize area as an attribute of plane figures and understand concepts of area measurement.
   a. A square with side length 1 unit, called "a unit square," is said to have "one square unit" of area, and can be used to measure area.
   b. A plane figure which can be covered without gaps or overlaps by n unit squares is said to have an area of n square units.
6. Measure areas by counting unit squares (square cm, square m, square in, square ft, and improvised units).
7. Relate area to the operations of multiplication and addition.
   a. Find the area of a rectangle with whole-number side lengths by tiling it, and show that the area is the same as would be found by multiplying the side lengths.
   b. Multiply side lengths to find areas of rectangles with whole number side lengths in the context of solving real-world and mathematical problems, and represent whole-number products as rectangular areas in mathematical reasoning.
   c. Use tiling to show in a concrete case that the area of a rectangle with whole-number side lengths a and $b + c$ is the sum of $a \times b$ and $a \times c$. Use area models to represent the distributive property in mathematical reasoning.

d. Recognize area as additive. Find areas of rectilinear figures by decomposing them into non-overlapping rectangles and adding the areas of the non-overlapping parts, applying this technique to solve real-world problems

And here are the standards for volume in grade five (5.MD.3–5):

Geometric measurement: understand concepts of volume and relate volume to multiplication and to addition.

3. Recognize volume as an attribute of solid figures and understand concepts of volume measurement.
   a. A cube with side length 1 unit, called a "unit cube," is said to have "one cubic unit" of volume, and can be used to measure volume.
   b. A solid figure which can be packed without gaps or overlaps using *n* unit cubes is said to have a volume of *n* cubic units.
4. Measure volumes by counting unit cubes, using cubic cm, cubic in, cubic ft, and improvised units.
5. Relate volume to the operations of multiplication and addition and solve real-world and mathematical problems involving volume.
   a. Find the volume of a right rectangular prism with whole-number side lengths by packing it with unit cubes, and show that the volume is the same as would be found by multiplying the edge lengths, equivalently by multiplying the height by the area of the base. Represent threefold whole-number products as volumes, e.g., to represent the associative property of multiplication.
   b. Apply the formulas $V = l \times w \times h$ and $V = b \times h$ for rectangular prisms to find volumes of right rectangular prisms with whole-number edge lengths in the context of solving real-world and mathematical problems.
   c. Recognize volume as additive. Find volumes of solid figures composed of two non-overlapping right rectangular prisms by adding the volumes of the non-overlapping parts, applying this technique to solve real-world problems.

The language is nearly identical in the two sets of standards. What is different is the concept: volume versus area, three-dimensional measurement versus two-dimensional measurement. This is a different form of spiral curriculum than the traditional type, in which a concept is introduced early and then repeated in greater depth. Here, the structure is repeated to show that the underlying concept is similar through more and more advanced stages of mathematics.

A review of the Common Core State Standards found that their coherence was similar to that of the highly regarded Singapore mathematics syllabus. In some cases, the review found, the Common Core Standards were even more explicit than Singapore's in showing the progression of topics across grades.[9]

Coherence Within Grades

In addition to showing coherence across grades by explicitly underscoring learning progressions to more advanced topics, the Standards also show coherence within grades through explicit links between concepts. The standards writers knew that, although the Standards are relatively lean compared to many previous state standards, teachers will want to combine them to teach them more efficiently. But they did not want to leave this work completely up to chance, and wanted to highlight some links that made sense conceptually.

Consider the third-grade standard for area shown earlier. It asks students to "relate area to the operations of multiplication and division," and expects them to use the arithmetic operations to solve measurement problems. In this way the standard makes clear the conceptual connection between area and multiplication, and helps teachers in creating lessons by enabling them to combine the topics. Similarly, as shown in chapter 2, the third-grade standards direct students to use bar graphs, a data topic, to underscore the concept of multiplication.

According to Jason Zimba, one of the lead authors of the mathematics standards, these connections are done judicially to highlight topics that have clear conceptual connections. They are not done for every topic. And some topics should not be linked. Zimba said he saw a textbook that had a chapter on "angles and order of operation." "That's not a thing," Zimba said.[10]

Putting Progressions into Practice

After the release of the Common Core State Standards, the mathematics writing team began developing draft documents to show the progression of learning implied by the standards for particular topics. The purpose of the documents, according to the project's Web site, was to link research and practice and to support teacher preparation, curriculum development, and textbook writing by explaining the organization of the standards, pointing out difficulties and pedagogical solutions, and giving more details on "particularly knotty areas" of mathematics.[11]

For instance, a draft document on geometry progressions for kindergarten through grade six outlines research on how children learn geometry and shows how the standards in that area for each grade build on children's knowledge and lead to a deeper understanding. At one point the document states: "The Standards for Kindergarten, Grade 1, and Grade 2 focus on three major aspects of geometry. Students build understandings of shapes and their properties, becoming able to do and discuss increasingly elaborate compositions, decompositions, and iterations of the two, as well as spatial structures and relations. In Grade 2, students begin the formal study of measure, learning to use units of length and use and understand rulers."[12]

Curriculum documents developed to be aligned with the Common Core State Standards show how the coherence in the Standards can support instruction. For example, a model curriculum developed by the Ohio Department of Education provides explicit connections between topics within a grade and across the grades to help teachers understand how their instruction on a particular topic supports attainment of standards, builds on student knowledge from prior years, and prepares them for the following year.

The model curriculum breaks down the Standards into "clusters" of content; for each cluster, the document provides suggested instructional strategies, resources, and common misconceptions. It also shows connections—to other topics within a grade level and to related topics in the previous and subsequent year.

For example, a sixth-grade section on the division of fractions by fractions (part of the number system) states that the topic is related to the cluster

"Connecting ratio and rate to whole number multiplication and division and using concepts of ratio and rate to solve problems," and provides a link to that cluster. The document also states that the fractions cluster "continues the work from Number and Operations in Base Ten and Number and Operations – Fractions," and that, in grade seven, it will be extended in The Number System to rational numbers and in Ratios and Proportional Reasoning.[13]

Progressions and Assessment

The learning progressions embedded in the Common Core State Standards can help teachers in developing and implementing formative assessments that check students' understanding throughout a school year. Teachers can design tasks that gauge where students are on the trajectory toward meeting the standards and can use instructional interventions to help students who are not yet meeting the standards.

Mathematics specialists at the Kentucky Department of Education have developed a series of formative assessment tasks aligned to the Common Core Standards. For instance, a third-grade task is designed to measure students' progress toward understanding fractions on a number line. This understanding is a key element in understanding fractions as numbers, a third-grade standard. Students first perform the task individually. In reviewing the responses, teachers can see whether students understand the concept or where their misconceptions lie. For example, students might place the fraction 3/4 between the number 3 and the number 4, thereby showing that they do not fully understand the distinction between fractions and whole numbers. Alternatively, students might order the fractions in increasing order on the line by the denominator (e.g., 1/3, 1/4, 1/5, 1/6), again showing a misunderstanding about fractions as units of a whole. Based on these responses, teachers then implement a lesson about swimmers in a race that are different fractions of the length of the pool. The students then discuss their responses in pairs. Finally, the students again try to place the fractions on a number line.

Teachers are able to interpret the student responses to the task because the coherence in the Common Core State Standards make clear the stages of learning that students take over time. An incorrect response might indicate that a student is at an earlier stage in learning, which gives teachers an idea of what to do to address the student's misconceptions.

However, the Standards do not indicate progressions of learning within grades. The order in which the standards appear does not specify a pathway teachers should follow; as the Standards document states, "Just because topic A [domain, in the Standards] appears before topic B in the standards for a given grade, it does not necessarily mean that topic A must be taught before topic B. A teacher might prefer to teach topic B before topic A, or might choose to highlight connections by teaching topic A and topic B at the same time. Or, a teacher might prefer to teach a topic of his or her own choosing that leads, as a byproduct, to students reaching the standards for topics A and B."[14]

But the coherence within grades can help teachers connect topics in ways that make sense mathematically. As noted earlier, for example, teachers in third grade can relate arithmetic operations to measurement by having students solve problems involving area.

The forthcoming Next Generation Science Standards, an effort led by Achieve that is separate from the Common Core Standards initiative, can also foster connections between mathematics and science. The NGSS indicate the mathematics standards from the Common Core that are related to a particular science standard. In that way, teachers can make connections across subject areas as well.

CHAPTER

4

An End to the Math Wars

During the 1990s, some of the most intense battles in education took place over how to teach mathematics. The weapons in the "math wars," as these disagreements were known, may have been words and ideas rather than implements of destruction, yet the combatants fought as ferociously as soldiers in any shooting war. And, some claimed, the wars produced some "collateral damage," with children and learning as the chief victims.

In essence, the math wars pitted those who argued for an emphasis on the ability of students to be able to use mathematics to solve real-world problems against those who argued for an emphasis on fluency in basic algorithms. But the battles touched on deeper topics as well, such as how children learn and how classrooms should be structured to foster student learning. These arguments reflected debates that went on in other subject areas as well.

The debates over math instruction played out in school board meetings, academic journals, and the popular press—and even in the halls of Congress. They affected state standards and multimillion-dollar decisions about textbooks and instructional materials. And, while results from the National Assessment of Educational Progress (NAEP) showed that student performance in mathematics improved substantially during the 1990s, the passion among the combatants did not abate for much of the decade.

The Common Core State Standards effectively imposed a cease-fire. This came about in part because mathematics educators recognized that they had more in common than their disagreements had seemed to suggest. But the Common Core also put an end to the math wars because, like any good agreement, it enabled each side to declare some measure of victory. In effect, the Standards stated that the wars were based on a false dichotomy: procedural fluency, conceptual understanding, and problem-solving abilities were *all* essential for all students.

The First Shot

Arguments about what to teach have long raged in American education. Educators have often been susceptible to fads that seem appealing but lack evidence of their effectiveness. And these new approaches have caused friction, especially with parents who rightfully take their children's education seriously and are often skeptical of teaching methods that appear to depart from how they were taught.

In reading, the most intense debates occurred between advocates of a phonics-based approach and those who favored methods that engaged students in reading literature from early ages—an approach often called "whole language." Those debates often grew vituperative; Rudolf Flesch's best-selling book *Why Johnny Can't Read* argued forcefully for the phonics emphasis and likened the whole-language advocates to Communists. The debate over reading continued well into the early twenty-first century.

Mathematics has had its share of debates as well. The curriculum materials produced in the wake of the Russian launch of the Sputnik satellite led to what was known as the "New Math," which introduced novel concepts like set theory and symbolic logic into the math curriculum. Teachers, unprepared for this way of teaching, failed to embrace the New Math, and parents were doubtful or worse. By the early 1970s, by most accounts, the New Math was "dead," replaced by a "back-to-basics" curriculum.

The first shot in the renewed and even more intense math wars took place in 1989, though few recognized it as such at the time. That year, the National Council of Teachers of Mathematics (NCTM) published *Curriculum and Evaluation Standards for School Mathematics,* which laid out a vision for mathematics instruction for all students (see chapter 1). The standards described in the NCTM document were intended to represent a consensus view of the mathematics education community, and they proved enormously influential, forming the basis for the standards that states were developing and for a revamped NAEP.

The NCTM *Standards* had a definite view about the way mathematics should be taught, representing a substantial shift from the back-to-basics approach. The document argued for much less emphasis on what mathematics educators called "shopkeeper arithmetic"—drills on conventional algorithms—and a much greater emphasis on conceptual understanding and the ability to solve problems that occurred in the real world. Gone, or almost gone, were long division, calculations of fractions using pencil and paper, and memorization of rules. In were the use of calculators, "operation sense," and the use of manipulative materials.

NCTM officials said these shifts were justified for several reasons. First, they noted, the growing availability of electronic tools like calculators and computers made paper-and-pencil calculating obsolete. Adults regularly used those tools to perform calculations at home and in the workplace; why shouldn't children learn to use them effectively in school?

Second, evidence from business showed that the workplace was changing. In part because of the availability of electronic tools, workers spent less and less time performing routine calculations. Instead, employers needed workers who were able to use their knowledge to solve non-routine problems. As the document put it, "Traditional notions of basic mathematical competence have been outstripped by ever-higher expectations of the skills and knowledge of workers . . . Employees must be prepared to understand the complexities and technologies of communication, to ask questions, to assimilate unfamiliar information, and to work cooperatively in teams. Businesses no longer seek workers with strong backs, clever hands, and 'shopkeeper' arithmetic skills."[1]

Third, emerging findings from cognitive science showed that students learned best when they were able to engage in projects and other activities that enabled them to use their knowledge actively. The type of instruction that characterized the back-to-basics classrooms, in which teachers lectured to students who sat silently and filled out worksheets, was less effective in fostering lasting and deep understanding, according to the cognitive scientists.

The *Standards* also reflected a desire among mathematics educators to delineate the mathematics necessary for all students, not just those who intended to pursue advanced mathematics coursework or technical careers. Data showed that the attrition in mathematics course-taking was sharp in high school, particularly among low-income students and students of color, and NCTM officials were concerned that the current trends foretold a division between a "technological elite" and a populace who lacked the understanding of mathematics needed for daily life. The curriculum suggested by the *Standards* was aimed at establishing a floor that would equip every student with a foundation in mathematics.

The War Is Joined

Although the NCTM document was clear about the direction the organization thought mathematics should take, the language it contained was often vague and general, and many educators read into the words more than they actually stated. Thus what followed from the NCTM *Standards* was not always what the NCTM had intended. As Alan H. Schoenfeld writes, "Because it was in essence a vision statement rather than a set of design specs, it proved remarkably enfranchising: During the coming years, different groups produced very different sets of materials 'in the spirit of the *Standards*.' And there is the rub. Some of the materials produced would be considered pretty flaky. Some of the classroom practices employed in the name of the *Standards* would appear pretty dubious. And the *Standards* would be blamed for all of them."[2]

The most vociferous reaction to the *Standards* and what it suggested about mathematics education emerged in California. This might have been expected. Beginning in the 1980s, under then–state superintendent of public instruction Bill Honig, California placed curriculum reform at the center of its educational agenda. Honig and his team produced curriculum frameworks—the beginnings of what we now call standards—in core subjects to guide instruction for all schools in the largest state. He also sought to use his state's size to leverage changes in textbooks, by requiring publishers to produce materials that conformed to the frameworks in order to be adopted for use statewide. Thus the changes in California would have national implications, since publishers hoped to sell the books that were produced for the California frameworks to a national market.

In 1992 the California Department of Education produced its mathematics framework (Honig was no longer superintendent, but his policy remained). It closely followed the NCTM blueprint, and in some ways went even farther than the national organization. For example, the California framework referred to calculators as "electronic pencils" and appeared to eschew paper-and-pencil calculations altogether.

And in response, publishers produced textbooks that departed sharply from previous materials. They organized lessons differently and included a variety of real-world settings for mathematics problems, such as the environment (leading some to call one book "Rainforest Algebra"). In addition, the state test that was intended to measure student performance against the curriculum framework also reflected the new approach. In one sample item that proved enormously controversial, students were asked to solve a problem and come up with a written justification for their answer. If the answer was correct and the justification weak, students received a low score; if the answer was incorrect and the justification was strong, students got a higher score.

The materials and tests sparked a noisy backlash, launching the math wars in earnest. Critics called the NCTM and California approaches "fuzzy math," and said they abandoned mathematics content. One group, calling itself Mathematically Correct, led the charge by creating a Web site to spread the word and organize political opposition to the new framework. They succeeded in persuading the state board of education to convene a panel to write a new framework in 1997, and they got the legislature to issue a directive to the panel requiring that any materials the panel adopted be based on "fundamental skills, including, but not limited to . . . basic computational skills."[3]

The skirmish drew national attention, with national educational leaders taking sides. Most of those who criticized the reform documents and sided with the more traditional approaches were political conservatives, such as Chester E. Finn Jr., the president of the Thomas B. Fordham Foundation, and Lynne V. Cheney, the former chairwoman of the National Endowment for the Humanities. But Senator Robert F. Byrd, a Democrat from West Virginia, also attacked the reformers. In a speech on the Senate floor, Byrd focused on the so-called "Rainforest Algebra" textbook and said:

> I took algebra instead of Latin when I was in high school. I never had this razzle-dazzle confusing stuff . . . This odd amalgam of math, geography, and language masquerading as an algebra textbook goes on to intersperse each chapter with helpful comments and photos of children named Taktuk, Esteban, and Minh . . . I still don't quite grasp the necessity for political correctness in an algebra textbook. Nor do I understand the inclusion of the United Nations Universal Declaration of Human Rights in three languages or a section on the language of algebra which defines such mathematically significant phrases as "the lion's share," the "boondocks," and "not worth his salt" . . . From there we hurry on to lectures on endangered species, a discussion of air pollution, facts about the Dogon people of West Africa, chili recipes and a discussion of varieties of hot peppers . . . what role zoos should play in today's society, and the dubious art of making shape images of animals on a bedroom wall, only reaching a discussion of the Pythagorean Theorem on page 502.[4]

Seeking Middle Ground

In response to the escalating rhetoric, U.S. Secretary of Education Richard Riley appeared before a group of mathematics associations in 1998 to plead for comity. And mathematics educators began to make what diplomats call "confidence-building gestures." For example, in 2000 the NTCM released a revised version of its *Standards* that increased the emphasis on computational skills. Although it did not go as far as its critics might have wanted, it showed the possibility of a middle ground.

Other mathematics educators also sought a truce. In 2003 Phil Daro, formerly director of the California Mathematics Project at the University of California, drafted a "Math Wars Peace Treaty" proposing that partisans on both sides accept that students should be fluent in computational skills *and* that they should be able to use mathematics to solve problems and be able to explain their reasoning. In an article in *Education Week,* Daro stated that skills, conceptual understanding, and problem-solving abilities are all necessary for all students, but the math wars had impeded efforts to bring an appropriate curriculum to schools. "Partisans in the math wars disagree about the causes of the problem (some preferring to focus on blame), and they disagree about the remedies. But they also agree on much, and particularly on the need for change. Ironically, the 'wars' hand victory to the status quo. Evidence from countries that perform well in mathematics shows that the war is phony. What's needed in mathematics is not one paradigm or another, but common-sense—and carefully engineered—changes in what we teach."[5]

Daro soon got the opportunity to put his ideas into practice. The Common Core State Standards initiative got under way in 2009, and Daro became one of the lead writers for the mathematics standards. The Standards would put an end to the math wars once and—educators hope—for all.

What the Standards Say

The Common Core State Standards state clearly that the goal of mathematics education is understanding: "These standards define what students should understand and be able to do in mathematics."[6] What is understanding? One way to determine if students understand mathematics, the document states, is to ask them to justify their solution to a problem. There is a "world of difference" between memorizing a method of solving a problem, it states, and explaining where the solution comes from. Moreover, students who can justify their approach are more likely than those who memorize it to be able to solve a less familiar problem.

The document goes on to state that "mathematical understanding and procedural skill are equally important, and both are assessable using mathematical tasks of sufficient richness."[7] That statement makes explicit the emphasis in the Standards on procedural fluency, conceptual understanding, and problem-solving. This emphasis begins as early as kindergarten. In that grade, students are expected to know number names and the count sequence, count to tell the number of objects, and compare numbers. They are also expected to understand addition as "putting together and adding to," and subtraction as "taking apart and taking from." And they are expected to classify objects and count the number of objects in categories—a rudimentary real-world problem.

The specific standards for understanding addition and subtraction further underline the focus on procedural knowledge, conceptual understanding, and problem-solving. Kindergartners are expected to "fluently add and subtract within 5; represent addition and subtraction with drawings, hand claps, and other means; and solve addition and subtraction word problems."

The three-part emphasis continues throughout the grades. In grade three, students are expected to "fluently multiply and divide within 100" (3.OA.7), and to know, from memory, all products of two one-digit numbers—the "times tables." They are also expected to identify arithmetic patterns (such as the fact that 4 times a number is always even) and to be able to explain these patterns using properties of operations. And they are expected to solve two-step word problems using the four arithmetic operations.

In grade five students are expected to write and interpret numerical expressions, understand place value, and graph points on the coordinate plane to solve real-world and mathematical problems. To demonstrate understanding of place value, students are expected to explain patterns in the number of zeros of the product when multiplying a number by powers of 10, and to explain patterns in the placement of the decimal point when a decimal is multiplied or divided by a power of 10. Fifth graders are also expected to fluently multiply multi-digit whole numbers using the standard algorithm.

By middle school, students are expected to deepen their understanding of mathematics concepts and to do more to apply their knowledge to solve problems. However, middle school continues the emphasis on procedural knowledge as well. For example, students in the seventh grade are expected to extend their knowledge of arithmetic with fractions to be able to add, subtract, multiply, and divide rational numbers.

In high school the emphasis shifts somewhat toward a greater focus on understanding and problem-solving. The assumption is that students already have mastered procedural fluency for much of elementary mathematics, and the Standards suggest that high school is the time to apply their knowledge. Thus the high school geometry standards state that students should be able to prove geometrical theorems, understand and apply theorems, and apply geometric concepts in modeling situations.

The Wars Resume

While the Standards were intended to end the math wars and present a consensus that procedural knowledge, conceptual understanding, and problem-solving were all important, some partisans refused to lay down their weapons. In a 2012 article on *The Atlantic* Web site, Barry Garelick, a scientist who has become a frequent commentator on mathematics education, criticized the Common Core State Standards for their call for conceptual understanding. He argued that students should know math facts fluently before being asked to explain them, and said that the Standards ask students to demonstrate their knowledge of math facts, such as adding and subtracting two- and three-digit numbers, later than they do in many state standards.

Garelick called the Standards' emphasis on balance "an odd pedagogical agenda, based on a belief that conceptual understanding must come before practical skills can be mastered. As this thinking goes, students must be able to explain the 'why' of a procedure. Otherwise, solving a math problem becomes a 'mere calculation' and the student is viewed as not having true understanding."[8]

But Hung-Hsi Wu, a professor emeritus of mathematics at the University of California, Berkeley, says the focus on teaching particular skills in early grades is precisely what was wrong with previous mathematics standards, and that the balance between knowledge and understanding is what the Common Core State Standards got right. In an article that could have been a response to Garelick (though it was written a year before), Wu writes:

> Indeed, the very purpose of mathematics standards (prior to the CCSS) seems to be to establish in which grade topics are taught. Often, standards are then judged by how early topics are introduced; thus, getting addition and subtraction of fractions done in fifth grade is taken as a good sign . . . The CCSS challenge this dogma. Importantly the CCSS do not engage in the senseless game of acceleration—to teach every topic as early as possible—even though the

> refusal to do so has been a source of some consternation in some quarters . . . But the real contribution of the CCSS lies in their insistence on righting the many wrongs in [traditional mathematics] . . . They are unique in their realization that the flaws in the logical development of [traditional mathematics]—not how early or how late each topic is placed in the standards—are the real impediment to any improvement in mathematics education. *Garbage in, garbage out,* as the saying goes. If we want students to learn mathematics, we have to teach it to them. Neither the previous mathematics standards nor the [traditional mathematics] on which they were based did that, but the CCSS do.[9]

Teaching for Fluency, Conceptual Understanding, and Problem-Solving

Teaching for fluency, conceptual understanding, and problem-solving is more time-consuming than focusing on just one of these competencies. Fortunately, the focus of the Standards (see chapter 2) affords teachers time to probe in depth on concepts, enabling students to develop an understanding and show that they can solve problems, not just apply algorithms. Instead of racing through an overcrowded curriculum, teachers can slow down and have students wrestle with each topic.

As Holly D. Zaluga-Alderete, a math teacher at Polk Middle School in Albuquerque, put it: "I don't have a mile-long list of standards to cover. For example, with the Pythagorean theorem, in the past, we would say, 'This is the Pythagorean theorem and how we use it' and move on. This year, we could get in depth, how it worked, the ins and outs . . . and knowing the whys."[10]

One approach that teachers are taking to implement this idea is to have students solve problems in multiple ways. That approach helps ensure that students are not simply following steps by rote, and that they understand what the problem asks and why their solution makes sense. In a Teaching Channel video, Jen Saul, a third-grade teacher at Aspire East Palo Alto Charter School in East Palo Alto, California, describes a method she uses called "Choose 3 Ways." In one example, students are presented with a problem: Four teachers have $20. Is that enough money for each of them to buy a burrito, which cost $4.12 each? And if they have enough for the burritos, do they have any money left over to buy sodas?

The students are then expected to write three possible solutions to the problem. According to Saul, if a student's solutions all come to the same answer, she can feel confident that she is correct. Saul then asks students to work together to share solutions. That, she says, provides students an opportunity to practice mathematical language. Finally, she allows a handful of students to present their solutions to the entire class. This step helps develop the culture of problem-solving in the class, she says. "It's not me dictating to them how to get to a particular result," Saul says.

This approach is similar to the approach used in Japan, according to researchers who led a study of classrooms using videotape. In a Japanese lesson, a teacher begins by reviewing the previous day's lesson, then introduces the problem of the day. Students work independently at their desks solving the problem; the teacher walks around the room and answers questions. Students then gather in groups to solve additional problems that are like the problem of the day. The teacher again circulates around the room, observing the groups' solutions. Only at the end of the class does the teacher suggest a solution.[11]

As Saul's experience shows, problem-solving begins in the primary grades; the Standards do not expect students to master procedures before they apply their knowledge to solve problems. Tasks on the Illustrative Mathematics Web site (a site created by the lead authors of the Common Core mathematics standards) show that problem-solving can begin as early as first grade. In one task, for second graders, students are given the following problem:

> Louis wants to give $15 to help kids who need school supplies. He also wants to buy a pair of shoes for $39.
>
> 1. How much money will he have to save for both?
> 2. Louis gets $5 a week for his allowance. He will save his allowance every week. How many weeks will it take him to reach this goal?
> 3. Louis remembers his sister's birthday is next month. He sets a goal of saving $16 for her gift. How many weeks will he have to save his allowance to reach this goal? How many weeks will he have to save his allowance for all three?

As the Web site's commentary on the task notes, this task combines procedural fluency with understanding and problem-solving. Students in second grade are expected to be able to add two-digit numbers fluently. They are also expected to develop their understanding of place value, and the addition of the $5 allowance supports that understanding. The problem also introduces an important real-world context, and it can be solved in several ways, by skip-counting or by creating a table to show the increase in income over time.

Assessments Measure All Three Abilities

The assessments being developed to measure student performance against the Common Core State Standards are expected to follow the Standards' lead and assess procedural fluency, conceptual understanding, and problem-solving abilities. This three-part emphasis is evident in the prototype test items released in 2012 by the Partnership for Assessment of Readiness for College and Careers (PARCC), one of the two state consortia developing the assessments (see chapter 1). For example, a sixth-grade item asks students to drag a slider across two parallel rulers, one that uses inches and the other that uses centimeters. The item asks students to select responses from among multiple choices that indicate the relationship between inches and centimeters, such as "The ratio of centimeters to inches is 1 to 2.54," "$c = 2.54i$, where i represents the number of inches and c represents the number of centimeters," and "For every inch, there are 2.54 centimeters." As these answers indicate, there is more than one correct answer; that item measures procedural knowledge.

Separate items measure students' conceptual understanding. One four-part task for sixth graders assesses students' understanding of rational numbers, including their understanding of rational numbers as points on a number line and of ordering and absolute value of rational numbers. The task describes a scale at a bakery that weighs cakes; those weighing more than 30 pounds are assigned a positive number (that is, a 33-pound cake would be 3), those below 30 pounds receive a negative number (a 27-pound cake would be −3), and those that are 30 pounds are assigned zero. The first part asks students to place cakes with assigned numbers on a number line. The second asks them to compare the weights of two cakes (students must understand that −3 is greater than −5). The third asks them to determine what the "reading with the largest absolute value" belongs to. And the fourth asks them to identify a cake with a reading that is more than 3 ounces above or below 30.

Other items measure students' ability to apply their knowledge to solve problems. A two-part task for seventh graders involves buying school supplies. In the first part, students must perform calculations to see if they can buy the supplies they need (with unit costs identified) with their available funds. The second tells them to fill bags for students with two pencils and thirty index cards each, when pencils are sold in packs of twelve and cards are sold in packs of 150, and asks how much each bag will cost. As the commentary on this task shows, students can approach this problem in several ways.

Sample items released by the Smarter Balanced Assessment Consortium show that this second consortium is also planning to measure procedural fluency, conceptual understanding, and problem-solving. One sample item suggests ways to measure procedural knowledge and understanding together. It states that a rectangle is 6 feet long and has a perimeter of 20 feet, and asks students to determine the width (procedural knowledge). It then asks students to explain how they got the answer (understanding).

These assessment items, like the classroom tasks earlier, represent a kind of peace treaty in the math wars.

CHAPTER

5

Covering All the Bases

MATHEMATICAL PRACTICES

In the past two decades, as educators have developed standards for what students should know and be able to do in core subjects, they have maintained that the practices of a discipline are at least as important as the content. That is, students should learn how mathematicians or scientists think, just as they learn the main ideas in each subject.

One of the most articulate expressions of this idea was a major report issued in 2012 intended to guide the development of standards in science. In that report, the National Research Council (NRC) laid out a three-part framework for K–12 education in science and engineering. This framework includes *practices,* or the methods of doing science; *cross-cutting concepts,* like energy and patterns, that are a part of all scientific disciplines; and *core ideas,* or the essential knowledge base of each discipline.

The report states that, by engaging in scientific practices and applying cross-cutting concepts to deepen their understanding of the core ideas, all graduating high school seniors will have acquired the basic knowledge and practical skills to become "critical consumers of scientific information related to their everyday lives" and to continue to learn science throughout their lives. The report notes that these goals are for all students, not just those intending to pursue scientific or technical careers.

The inclusion of practices as a key component of the framework is significant. It signals that the consensus committee that produced the report believes that science is not just a collection of unrelated facts. Rather, it is also a way of looking at and organizing the world to make sense of those facts. Only by engaging in the practices can students truly learn science, the report argues. As it states: "Science is not just a body of knowledge that reflects current understanding of the world; it is also a set of practices used to establish, extend, and refine that knowledge. Both elements—knowledge and practice—are essential."[1]

This point of view has attracted some controversy. Some critics contend that equating practices and core ideas downgrades the content of science, and have expressed concerns that students might end up not knowing much science as a result. But the NRC committee was clear that practices and core ideas are intertwined, and that the science standards that are being written to conform to the framework will include both components.

The Common Core State Standards in mathematics, released two years earlier than the NRC science framework, likewise include standards for mathematical practices as well as standards for mathematical content. As with the science framework, the inclusion of these practices is intended to convey the idea that doing mathematics is as important as knowing concepts and skills; indeed, students can only learn the mathematical ideas through the practices. And as with the framework, the math standards have attracted controversy for this point as well. But the inclusion of the practices could lead to significant changes in how mathematics is taught.

A Focus on Process

The idea of standards for mathematical practices is not new. The National Council of Teachers of Mathematics' *Curriculum and Evaluation Standards for School Mathematics,* originally published in 1989, included four standards for mathematical processes for each grade band (K–4, 5–8, 9–12): mathematics as problem-solving, mathematics as communication, mathematics as reasoning, and mathematical connections. In fact, in the original document, the process standards were placed before the standards for mathematical content, which focused on areas such as numbers and operations, geometry, functions, and so forth. As one commenter noted, "Epistemologically, with its focus on process, the *Standards* could be seen as a challenge to the 'content-oriented' view of mathematics that predominated for more than a century."[2]

The inclusion of the process standards underscored the emphasis in the NCTM document on ensuring that students developed the ability to use their knowledge to solve problems and communicate effectively. Critics expressed concern that the process standards downplayed content or ignored it altogether, and some said the result was "fuzzy math" (see chapter 4).

A subsequent revision of the NCTM standards in 2000 reversed the order of the standards, placing the content standards first, but it continued to include the four process standards from the earlier document and in fact added one more, on representation, which emphasizes understanding ways that mathematical ideas are represented through pictures, tables, graphs, number and letter symbols, and so forth. The document states: "When students gain access to mathematical representations and the ideas they express, and when they can create representations to capture mathematical concepts or relationships, they acquire a set of tools that significantly expand their capacity to model and interpret physical, social, and mathematical phenomena."[3]

The idea of incorporating mathematical practices into instruction was supported by an influential NRC report from 2001 that outlined what was known about teaching mathematics in elementary school. The report, entitled *Adding It Up,* defined mathematics proficiency as consisting of five strands. Three of the strands involved knowledge and skills in mathematical content: conceptual understanding, procedural fluency, and strategic competence (thus anticipating the Common Core Standards' solution to the "math wars"—see chapter 4). The other two represented practices or processes: adaptive reasoning, which included reflection, explanation, and justification; and productive dispositions, which included a sense of efficacy and a belief in diligence.[4] The report noted that these strands are intertwined, and thus have implications for how teachers teach mathematics and how students learn it.

The Processes in Practice

As the 2012 NRC report suggests, applying the practices in classrooms has changed instruction. Stephanie Smith, Marvin Smith, and Thomas Romberg describe a classroom in which students engaged in active discussions about ways to determine the relationship between U.S. dollars and Dutch guilders and ways to represent this relationship mathematically. Students propose rules to describe the relationship mathematically, and the teacher, without commenting, asks students if the students' rules are reasonable. The authors conclude: "With his questioning, [the teacher] orchestrated a rich, problem-solving discussion about a genuine dilemma that had arisen for his students. Rather than finding correct answers to routine exercises, he emphasized the process of solving the dilemma at hand as well as understanding mathematical concepts. The experiences also provided opportunities to make mathematical connections during future discussions."[5]

Yet data from national and international assessments show that these changes have not been widespread. On the Programme for International Student Assessment (PISA), for example, a test that measures fifteen-year-old students' ability to apply their knowledge to solve real-world problems, U.S. students have consistently scored well below their peers from other countries. In 2009, for example, U.S. fifteen-year-olds ranked twenty-fifth among industrialized countries in mathematical problem-solving, at about the same level as Portugal and Italy.

In addition, results from the National Assessment of Educational Progress (NAEP) show that while U.S. students can perform basic mathematical procedures, few can apply their knowledge to solve problems. Only 35 percent of eighth graders, for example, performed at the proficient level in mathematics on NAEP in 2011, a level that indicates that students can "apply mathematical concepts and procedures consistently to complex problems."[6]

These assessment results confirm findings from observational studies of U.S. classrooms showing that, in many cases, teachers focus on procedures rather than on problem-solving and communication. One well-known study, conducted to accompany the Third International Mathematics and Science Study (TIMSS) in 1995, was based on videotapes of a hundred eighth-grade classrooms in Germany, fifty classrooms in Japan, and eighty-one in the United States. The researchers found stark differences among the countries, but fairly consistent patterns within them. "What we can see clearly," write James Stigler and James Hiebert, "is that American mathematics teaching is extremely limited, focused for the most part on a very narrow band of procedural skills. Whether students are in rows working individually or sitting in groups, whether they have access to the latest technology or are working only with paper and pencil, they spend most of their time acquiring isolated skills through repeated practice."[7] By contrast, they note, "Japanese classrooms spend as much time solving challenging problems and discussing mathematical concepts as they do practicing skills."[8]

Clearly, the mathematical practices outlined in the NCTM standards have failed to pervade American schools on a large scale. Problem-solving, communication, reasoning, and mathematical connections remain rare, and the epistemological upheaval that the NCTM document purported to undertake has not taken place.

The Eight Mathematics Practice Standards in the Common Core

The Common Core State Standards for Mathematics lists eight standards for mathematical practices:

1. *Make sense of problems and persevere in solving them.* Mathematically proficient students begin by trying to understand the meaning of a problem and plan a solution before diving in. They monitor their progress and change course if necessary, and check their answers.
2. *Reason abstractly and quantitatively.* Mathematically proficient students can both decontextualize problems—convert a problem into abstract symbols and manipulate them—and contextualize problems—understand what symbols refer to.

3. *Construct viable arguments and critique the reasoning of others.* Mathematically proficient students justify their conclusions and explain them to others, understand and refute counterclaims, and evaluate the arguments of others.
4. *Model with mathematics.* Mathematically proficient students apply their mathematical knowledge to problems arising in real life.
5. *Use appropriate tools strategically.* Mathematically proficient students determine what tools apply to a particular situation. Tools can include pencil and paper, rulers, spreadsheets, or geometry software.
6. *Attend to precision.* Mathematically proficient students are careful about the language and symbols they use to explain their solutions.
7. *Look for and make use of structure.* Mathematically proficient students look closely to determine the structure of a problem, and see if they can convert a complex thing, such as an algebraic expression, into a single one.
8. *Look for and express regularity in repeated reasoning.* Mathematically proficient students try to discern patterns and look for methods that would apply generally or shortcuts to solving problems.

These standards stand apart—physically in the document as well as conceptually—from the content standards that make up the bulk of the expectations for student performance for each grade. The document begins with an explanation of the standards for mathematical practice, and the eight standards are listed with each set of grade-level content standards, although off to the side.

In addition, there are conceptual differences between the content and practice standards. For example, whereas the content standards vary by grade level, to provide a progression of knowledge and skills over time (see chapter 3), the practice standards are the same for every grade. However, the document notes that students' mastery of the practice standards should develop over time: "The Standards for Mathematical Practice describe ways in which developing student practitioners of the discipline of mathematics increasingly ought to engage with the subject matter as they grow in mathematical maturity and expertise throughout the elementary, middle, and high school years."[9]

The document further states that the practice standards should be integrated with the content standards, although it suggests that it is the role of the designers of curriculum, assessments, and professional development to make those connections. Standards that begin with the word "understand" are a good place to link content and practice standards, the document states, since understanding is likely to lead students to represent problems coherently, justify their conclusions, use technology appropriately, and explain their understanding to others.

One exception to the separateness of the content and practice standards is Standard 4, Model with Mathematics. At the high school level, modeling is a content standard, along with number, algebra, functions, and geometry. Modeling, the document states, "is the process of choosing and using appropriate mathematics and statistics to analyze empirical situations, to understand them better, and to improve decisions."[10] Some examples include analyzing the stopping distance for a car; modeling savings account balances or bacterial growth; or analyzing risk in situations such as extreme sports, pandemics, and terrorism.

The modeling cycle, the document states, involves six steps: identifying variables; formulating a model; analyzing and performing operations to draw a conclusion; interpreting the results; validating the conclusions; and reporting the results.

While modeling remains a separate standard within the high school standards, there are no substandards for modeling, as there are for the content standards. As the document states, "Modeling is best interpreted not as a collection of isolated topics but rather in relation to other standards."[11] Instead, the document uses an asterisk to identify substandards within the content standards in which modeling applies. One such standard is a function standard: "Write arithmetic and geometric sequences both recursively and with an explicit formula, use them to model situations, and translate between the two forms" (F-BF.2). Another is this algebra standard: "Derive the formula for the sum of a finite geometric series (when the common ratio is not 1), and use the formula to solve problems. *For example, calculate mortgage payments*" (A-SSE.4; emphasis in original).

Putting the Practice Standards into Practice

The standards for practice are intended to be integrated with the content standards; teachers implementing the Common Core State Standards typically embed them in their units and tasks designed to teach and assess the content standards. One would be unlikely to see lessons aimed at teaching the practice standards by themselves.

One area where the practice standards come into play most vividly is in assessments. The tasks that students are asked to perform to demonstrate their procedural knowledge, conceptual understanding, and problem-solving abilities can also be designed to enable them to demonstrate their habits of mind and dispositions. The assessments now being developed to measure student performance against the Common Core State Standards might provide some indications of how students perform on the practices, although at the time of this writing the way the results will be reported has not been determined. The two consortia developing Common Core assessments are using a process known as evidence-centered design, in which the consortia develop items and tasks that will provide evidence regarding the "claims" they want to make about student performance. Draft claims developed by the Smarter Balanced Assessment Consortium show that the assessment will provide evidence about concepts and procedures, problem-solving, communicating reasoning, and modeling and data analysis. The Partnership for the Assessment of Readiness for College and Careers, meanwhile, proposes five claims about student performance in mathematics that emphasize a connection between content and mathematical practices; two of the claims highlight specific practice standards—expressing mathematical reasoning and modeling.

Sample tasks that have been released by the two assessment consortia show how the standards for practice can be integrated with the content standards. For example, one fourth-grade task developed for PARCC by the Charles A. Dana Center at the University of Texas at Austin shows students three types of vehicles—buses, vans, and cars—and indicates how many passengers each can hold. It then says that three classes at Lakeview School want to go on a field trip, and indicates how many students are in each class. It then asks the students to determine the combination of vehicles needed to transport the students from the three classes on the trip.

A commentary on the task shows the standards this task measures. In addition to the content standards of number and operations ("use place value understanding and properties of operations to solve multi-digit arithmetic") and operations and algebraic thinking ("use the four operations with whole numbers to solve problems"), the task also involves the first two practice standards. Because there are multiple entry points into a solution, the problem requires students to formulate a solution pathway. In addition, there are multiple correct answers, so students must persevere to reach all the possible solutions, thus meeting the first standard, *Make sense of problems and persevere in solving them.*

The task also addresses the second practice standard, *Reason abstractly and quantitatively,* because it requires students to think about their calculations in the abstract, to manipulate numbers, and then to place the numbers back into the real-world context to assess the reasonableness of their answers.

A task that addresses the third practice standard, *Construct viable arguments and critique the reasoning of others,* asks students to justify their conclusions and communicate them to others, and to anticipate and address counterarguments. Thus, in addition to providing a solution, students must also explain their solution and show why it is correct. In a webinar sponsored by the Math and Science Partnership, Deborah Loewenberg Ball, the dean of the school of education at the University of Michigan, described one addition to a simple arithmetic task that addresses this standard. The problem states that a student has in his pocket pennies, nickels, and dimes, and pulls out two coins, then asks how much money he has in his hands. To enable students to construct and analyze arguments, Ball adds an additional question: Prove that you have all possible solutions. By answering that question, students must come up with reasonable mathematical arguments, and students can critique them using mathematical reasoning.

The fourth practice standard, *Model with mathematics*, requires students to apply mathematics to real-world situations. Unlike with textbook problems, which typically ask students to apply the mathematical topic that was just taught, students in real-world situations need to figure out which type of mathematics applies to a particular problem. They also need to make appropriate assumptions, sift through data and determine which data are relevant, and construct a mathematical solution.

Thus tasks that address modeling present information and ask students to apply their mathematical knowledge to determine not only the answer, but how to solve it. For example, consider the following seventh-grade task:

Four different stores are having a sale. The signs below show the discounts available at each of the four stores.

Two for the price of one
Buy one and get 25% off the second
Three for the price of one
Buy two and get 50% off the second

1. Which of these four different offers gives the biggest percentage price reduction? Explain your reasoning clearly.
2. Which of these four different offers gives the smallest percentage price reduction? Explain your reasoning clearly.

To solve this problem, students must make assumptions about the price of various items, use appropriate mathematical procedures (arithmetic, fractions, percentages, algebra) to solve it, and show why their solution is reasonable.

The fifth practice standard, *Use appropriate tools strategically*, is similar to the modeling standard in that it asks students to make judgments about which tools are appropriate, rather than having that information provided to them. That is, students need to determine when a calculator is called for (for example, in a problem involving graphing of functions) and when it is not (in making estimates to determine whether a particular solution is reasonable).

The sixth practice standard, *Attend to precision,* means more than coming up with the right answer. It also involves using symbols correctly and communicating in precise terms to others. A fifth-grade task that addresses this standard asks students to analyze a set of mathematical expressions that use the same numbers, but with parentheses in different places. To solve it, students need to know what parentheses represent and why they affect the order of operations.

The seventh practice standard, *Look for and make use of structure,* asks students to step back from solving problems to discern patterns. In doing so, students develop a deeper understanding of the mathematics underlying the problems. For example, in a task that asks young students to add three things to seven things and then to add seven things to three things, children not only can come up with the answer, but also look for ways the pattern might apply to other sets of numbers.

Students can also use a variety of approaches to come up with structures. In her webinar, Deborah Ball described a problem that asked students to use the numeral 8 and the + sign to come up with as many equations as possible for the number 1,000. (Solutions included 8 + 8 + 8 . . . , 888 + 88 + 8 . . . , etc.) By creating a table, she said, students can see that the number of addends in each equation varied by 10, thus pointing to a possible mathematical rule.

The final standard of practice, *Look for and express regularity in repeated reasoning,* takes the seventh standard and goes a step further by asking students to use the patterns they identify to come up with mathematical solutions. One sixth-grade task that addresses this is known as "the Djinn's Offer." It states that a Djinn appears on a desert island to offer a student a choice: she can have a coin worth $50,000, or a magic coin that doubles in value every day. To determine which is the better offer, students must use repeated reasoning to determine exponential value.

Preparing Teachers

In her webinar, Deborah Ball said that the centrality of the standards for mathematical practice in the Common Core State Standards represents a substantial shift for many teachers, and that teachers need to develop their knowledge and skills in order to enable students to meet those standards. She suggested ways that teacher education programs and professional development could support teachers in making this shift.

First, she noted, teachers need to develop their own knowledge about the practices and how they apply in classrooms. To do so, teachers need to solve mathematical problems themselves and understand the practices involved in solving them. They also need to study their students and see the practices they use to solve problems. And they need to develop instructional strategies to help students understand the practices; for example, teachers need to establish structures for students to develop explanations, not simply to let them solve the problems on their own. The classroom described by Smith, Smith, and Romberg, in which students proposed rules for the relationship between dollars and Dutch guilders, exemplifies this principle.

In addition, Ball said, teachers need to see that all students are capable of applying the standards of mathematical practice. These standards are not something extra, once students have mastered basic skills. Teachers can see this by viewing videos of English language learners and other underserved groups of students applying the standards, she suggested.

Ball also said that teachers need to understand that the Common Core State Standards, by including the standards of practice, have broadened the conception of mathematical competence. According to Ball, the standards of practice are part of what it means to be a mathematically proficient student. "The practices are basic to the content of mathematics, not just part of the means," she added. "This is a reconceptualization of what we mean by basic skills."[12]

CHAPTER

6

Just the Facts

In 2010, the California Partnership for Achieving Student Success (Cal-PASS) found that 74 percent of students from a San Diego public high school who earned grades of A or B in their high school English classes did not pass their English placement exams upon entering community college and were assigned to remedial courses. The remediation rates were high whether students stopped taking English classes after tenth grade or continued through twelfth grade.

Looking deeper, Cal-PASS found that the problem was what was being taught: high school and community college teachers were teaching different curricula. While the high school program reflected the national emphasis on literature, focusing on characters and story lines, the community college teachers focused on writing to inform, persuade, and describe.[1] In response to this finding, high school teachers revamped their instruction; 86 percent of graduates then were able to enter college and go right into credit-bearing English courses and complete them successfully.

One of the key motivating factors in the development of the Common Core State Standards was the apparent mismatch between what schools teach and what students are expected to be able to do in college and the workplace. Researchers had found that students who performed as expected in high school had to take remedial coursework when they arrived at college, and many students who take remedial courses in college fail to graduate.

But research shows that the mismatch between the school literacy curriculum and the expectations for post-secondary education actually begins much earlier than high school. As early as the primary grades, the overwhelming majority of what students read are narrative texts, and much of their writing is narrative. Informational texts, the kind students will increasingly read after they leave high school, are relatively rare. Without a shift in the emphasis on narrative reading and writing, students will find themselves not ready for postsecondary success.

The Common Core State Standards aim to close that gap. The Standards call for a much greater emphasis on nonfiction texts—50 percent in elementary school and 70 percent in high school—and a strong emphasis on expository writing. Not all of these texts are expected to be read in English classes; the Standards make clear that students should read and write in every class. Nevertheless, these expectations will lead to substantial shifts in curriculum and instruction in many schools.

The Stable Canon

Although there has been little recent research on the books assigned in high school English classes, studies from the late 1980s and early 1990s show that the high school English curriculum is fairly consistent across the United States. A major survey of nearly five hundred schools, conducted in 1988, found that the top ten assigned books were similar in public, Catholic, and independent schools. The most frequently required titles in grades nine through twelve in public schools were:

1. Romeo and Juliet
2. Macbeth
3. Huckleberry Finn
4. Julius Caesar
5. To Kill a Mockingbird
6. The Scarlet Letter
7. Of Mice and Men
8. Hamlet
9. The Great Gatsby
10. Lord of the Flies

Independent schools were more likely to assign *The Odyssey*, but otherwise the top ten in each type of schools included the same titles.[2]

Moreover, the makeup of the list as a whole changed little over the previous few decades. Compared with a similar survey conducted in 1963, the 1988 study found a slight increase in the proportion of works written by women (19 percent compared with 17 percent), and a slight increase in works written by alternative cultural traditions (2 percent, compared with 0.6 percent). However, the 1988 list included more U.S. authors and fewer British authors.

A similar study of anthologies used in English classes in grades seven through ten, conducted in 1989, found a few shifts over time in the materials included. The study found that nearly all teachers use anthologies, and about two-thirds of teachers surveyed said the books were their primary source of materials. Compared with a similar survey conducted in 1961, the 1989 survey found more works by women and minorities (although their representation was still small), and fewer contemporary works.

One of the most significant findings of the 1989 anthology study was a steep decline in nonfiction works. Although nonfiction works were more prevalent in anthologies used in high school than in those used in middle grades, the proportion of nonfiction titles included in anthologies as a whole dropped from 26 percent in 1961 to 13 percent in 1989.[3]

Informational texts are significantly underrepresented in elementary schools as well. A 2010 study of first-grade classrooms by Nell K. Duke, now a professor of language, literacy, and culture at the University of Michigan College of Education, found that only 9.8 percent of books and other materials in classroom libraries, and a mere 2.6 percent of materials on classroom walls, were informational text. In addition, she found that only 3.6 minutes of the classroom day were devoted to informational text—only 1.9 minutes in classrooms with students from low socioeconomic backgrounds.[4]

Other studies showed a similar imbalance between narrative and informational texts in elementary schools. One study of first-grade basal readers submitted for adoption in Texas found that only 12 percent of the selections were nonfiction. A separate study of second-grade basal readers found that 16 percent of the selections were informational. A national survey of exemplary primary reading teachers found that only 6 percent of the material read in their classrooms was expository. And a study of materials read at home to kindergarten children found that only 7 percent of the books parents read to children were informational.[5]

These patterns have had significant consequences for students' interest in and ability to read informational texts. One survey of seventh graders found that 80 percent of the students disliked reading informational texts, and nearly half said they try to get out of reading them for school. Significantly, higher-achieving students were more likely than lower-achieving students to dislike informational texts. Why? The survey's authors suggest their attitude might reflect the heavy emphasis on fiction in elementary schools.

> It is conceivable that this repulsion toward information text is due to the near total reliance on literature for teaching reading in the elementary grades. Students learn to read words and gain comprehension skills in the context of stories. Basal readers in elementary school and middle school are almost totally fiction and literature, with a few exceptions for biography and the occasional piece of science text. Students who are successful in reading enjoy these stories, and those who derive the most satisfaction from literature are likely to read more and increase their competency. Thus, competency in reading is associated with enjoyment of fiction.[6]

The emphasis on narrative texts also affects students' ability to read informational texts. On the 2003 Progress in International Reading Literacy Study (PIRLS), American ten-year-olds had the largest gap in performance between literary reading and informational reading of any country participating in the assessment. In the 2011 PIRLS assessment, the results were similar.

Elementary teachers might have downplayed informational texts because they believed that their focus should be on teaching children decoding skills and reading fluency, or because they believed that informational texts were too difficult for young children. But research shows that these beliefs are misguided, Duke says. First graders who read informational texts had decoding and spelling skills comparable to similar students who lacked exposure to such texts. And many studies have found that children as young as three are capable of reading informational text.[7] Rather than avoid informational texts, Duke says, elementary teachers should increase students' exposure to them to provide the students with real-world information on real-world experiences, and to do so in contexts that are motivating to children.

Duke and others note that informational texts also help improve students' reading abilities more generally. For one thing, informational texts help students develop the background knowledge they need to read other texts. Researchers have found that background knowledge is a critical factor in comprehension; as an influential National Research Council report pointed out, "Knowledge of the content addressed by a text plays an important part in the reader's formation of the text's main ideas and can be traded off to some extent against weak word-recognition skills."[8] In addition to content knowledge, informational texts also build vocabulary, another critical factor in comprehension.

Researchers have also found that informational texts help motivate students to read by exciting their interests. Although many students find fiction appealing, many others are intrigued by the topics they read in informational texts, and they are more likely to read such texts if given the choice.[9] This is particularly important for boys, who tend to perform less well than girls in reading. Boys are enthusiastic about nonfiction and informational texts; however, most of the informational texts they encounter in school are textbooks, which, as the survey of seventh graders mentioned earlier found, turn students off to reading. Stimulating nonfiction articles and texts about topics that interest them can motivate boys to read more.[10]

Most encouragingly, informational texts also help improve reading comprehension. Studies of elementary science programs that use informational texts found that students improved not only their science achievement but their reading achievement as well. Similarly, studies of a content-based program of instruction for middle schoolers found significant improvements in reading ability.[11]

There are efforts under way to increase the emphasis on informational texts at all grade levels. The National Assessment of Educational Progress (NAEP) includes a substantial proportion of informational texts in its assessments. The NAEP Reading framework for the 2011 assessment proposed that informational texts comprise 50 percent of the reading passages for fourth grade, 55 percent of the passages for eighth grade, and 70 percent of the passages for twelfth grade. The remainder would be narrative texts, although the framework notes that some of the texts could be literary nonfiction, which includes aspects of both genres.[12] The framework document notes that comprehension of these texts is essential because adults read predominantly informational texts.

Similarly, the NAEP writing assessment framework places the majority of its emphasis on informational writing. At fourth grade, 30 percent of tasks would be persuasive, 35 percent explanatory, and 35 percent to convey experience (real or imagined). At eighth grade, 35 percent of the tasks would be persuasive, 35 percent explanatory, and 30 percent to convey experience. At twelfth grade, 40 percent of the tasks would be persuasive, 40 percent explanatory, and 20 percent to convey experience. As the document notes, the proportion of persuasive and explanatory texts is higher than in the previous NAEP framework, reflecting the revised expectations for youths' postsecondary writing.[13]

What the Standards Say

The Common Core State Standards follow the NAEP framework. As the document states, "The Standards aim to align instruction with this framework so that many more students than at present can meet the requirements of college and career readiness. In K–5, the Standards follow NAEP's lead in balancing the reading of literature with the reading of informational texts. . . . In accord with NAEP's growing emphasis on informational texts in the higher grades, the Standards demand that a significant amount of reading of informational texts take place."[14]

However, the same paragraph that sets forth those requirements also notes that much of the nonfiction reading will be done *outside of English language arts class*. As the Standards state, "Because the ELA classroom must focus on literature (stories, drama, and poetry) as well as literary nonfiction, a great deal of informational reading in grades 6–12 must take place in other classes if the NAEP assessment framework is to be matched instructionally." A footnote further spells this out: "The percentages on the table reflect the sum of student reading, not just reading in ELA settings. Teachers of senior English classes, for example, are not required to devote 70 percent of reading to informational texts. Rather, 70 percent of student reading across the grade should be informational."[15]

Similarly, the Standards call for a greater emphasis on expository and persuasive writing as opposed to narrative. As noted above, the 2011 NAEP writing framework states that the amount of writing in all three genres should be distributed roughly equally in fourth and eighth grade, but by twelfth grade persuasive and expository writing would expand to 40 percent each, with the remaining 20 percent assigned to conveying experience.

As the Standards document states, these shifts are consistent with the requirements for college and careers. "Evidence concerning the demands of college and career readiness gathered during development of the Standards concurs with NAEP's shifting emphases: standards for grades 9–12 describe writing in all three forms, but, consistent with NAEP, the overwhelming focus of writing throughout high school should be on arguments and informative/explanatory texts."[16] A footnote points out that the proportions include writing in all subject areas, not solely English language arts.

David Coleman, one of the lead authors of the English language arts standards, expressed the importance of the shift toward expository writing in blunt form to a meeting of New York educators in 2011: a boss, he said, would never tell an employee, "Johnson, I need a market analysis by Friday, but before that, I need a compelling account of your childhood."[17]

The End of Literature?

The Standards' proposal to increase the amount of informational texts and expository writing has sparked some heated reaction. In a playful tone, Alexandra Petri, a humor columnist for the *Washington Post,* said the requirements would force students to abandon literature and read government documents instead: "Forget *Catcher in the Rye* (seems to encourage assassins), *The Great Gatsby* (too 1 percenty), *Huckleberry Finn* (anything written before 1970 must be racist) and *To Kill a Mockingbird* (probably a Suzanne Collins rip-off). Bring out the woodchipping manuals!"[18]

In a more serious vein, the Pioneer Institute, a Boston-based organization that has been sharply critical of the Common Core Standards, released a report in September 2012 arguing that the emphasis on informational text would reduce students' college readiness. The report stated that there is no research to support the Standards' proposal for a high proportion of informational text, and noted that in Massachusetts, where standards call for 60 percent literary texts and 40 percent informational texts, students demonstrated the highest performance in the nation in reading.[19]

These articles and reports caused consternation among teachers, but the critics may have misunderstood the Standards. The critics contended that the Standards' proposals would cause English teachers to abandon literature in favor of nonfiction texts like "woodchipping manuals." In fact, as noted above, the Standards document states explicitly that the proportion of informational texts and expository writing called for in the Standards represents all of a student's time, not just the time in English class. The Standards make clear that students should read informational texts in social studies, science, and technical subjects, such as career-education classes, as well.

The misinformation about the Standards has extended to the text suggestions included in the Standards' supporting documents. Although the Standards themselves do not prescribe a reading list, the English Language Arts Appendix B includes a list of texts that are intended to show representative works of appropriate complexity for each grade level. As we will see in chapter 8, the Standards stress the ability of students to read texts of increasing complexity, and lay out a method of assessing complexity to ensure that students are on track toward reading the works that they will encounter after high school.

The list of suggestions in the Language Arts appendix includes a wide range of works. For grades six through eight, the list includes *The Adventures of Tom Sawyer, Little Women,* and Langston Hughes's poem *I, Too, Sing America.* But the list also includes informational texts, such as *Narrative of the Life of Frederick Douglass,* the Preamble and First Amendment to the United States Constitution, and Henry Petrosky's "The Evolution of the Grocery Bag." The list also includes the *Invasive Plant Inventory*, from the California Invasive Plant Council.

In her satire of the reading requirements, Alexandra Petri pointed to the *Invasive Plant Inventory* as one of the manuals that would elbow out Mark Twain in English classes. But the list makes clear that these suggested works are intended for science, mathematics, and technical subjects, not English. English classes are safe for Mark Twain. And in any event, these suggested works are intended to be illustrative, not a required reading list.

The Standard in Practice

As the language in the Standards document makes clear, much of the responsibility for meeting the requirement for a greater proportion of nonfiction texts rests with teachers of science, social studies, and technical subjects. As chapter 10 will show, the Standards are likely to lead to a greater emphasis on reading and writing across the curriculum in middle and high school, in order to ensure that students meet the literacy standards for the content areas.

In elementary school, the Standards' emphasis on nonfiction might encourage schools to increase their focus on subjects other than reading and mathematics. This would represent a shift from current practice. Over the past decade, as No Child Left Behind measured schools' performance solely on the basis of tests in reading and mathematics, a number of elementary schools have reduced time spent on social studies and science. A study by the Center on Education Policy found that 36 percent of districts had reduced time for social studies, by an average of 76 minutes per week, and 28 percent had reduced time for science, by an average of 75 minutes per week.[20] But if half the reading that elementary students do is expected to be nonfiction, then schools might have an incentive to increase the amount of instruction in science and social studies and provide students opportunities to read textbooks and historical documents.

The nonfiction requirement also creates opportunities for cross-disciplinary connections. For example, Erika Parker, a preschool teacher in Baltimore, had her four- and five-year-olds read *The Three Little Pigs* in advance of a visit to a farm. But the students also read stories about fall weather, the life cycle of a pumpkin, and how to grow apples. As noted by her district's chief academic officer, Sonja B. Santelises, such informational texts are essential to build the content knowledge all students need in order to comprehend literature. This is particularly important for students who seldom visit museums or who lack books at home.[21]

What will happen in English language arts classrooms? In many cases, nothing: as noted earlier, teachers will continue to teach Shakespeare and Mark Twain. But teachers will also likely introduce some nonfiction documents into instruction, not to teach them for their historical or scientific information, but to teach them as *literature*. That is, teachers will engage classrooms in examinations of the rhetorical and textual features of nonfiction works, to see how writers use language and syntax to explain and persuade.

For example, teachers might want to teach the literary aspects of some of the founding documents of the United States, such as the Declaration of Independence, to show how the Founders employed a deft use of persuasive language to make their case for separation from the British Empire. Similarly, a lesson plan from the Library of Congress suggests that teachers can teach Lincoln's second inaugural address as a work of literature. Students could examine questions such as: What themes emerge? What was Lincoln's purpose? How did this address compare with Lincoln's first inaugural address? How did it compare with other presidential inaugural addresses?[22] Likewise, a text such as Dr. Martin Luther King Jr.'s "Letter from Birmingham Jail" provides ample opportunities to show how a writer can construct an argument to make a powerful case for action in the face of resistance.

These texts can also help schools integrate instruction across classrooms. For example, students can read Lincoln's second inaugural address while studying the Civil War and Reconstruction in social studies; or they can read "Letter from Birmingham Jail" in English classes while studying the civil rights movement in history. Likewise, English teachers can focus on a book such as *The Worst Hard Time,* by Timothy Egan, while science teachers teach lessons on drought and crop rotation and social studies teachers address the Great Depression and the New Deal.

In upper grades, the growing body of literary nonfiction works—like *The Worst Hard Time*—offer ample opportunities for study of the literary techniques involved in writing nonfiction. Such books often employ character development and structural elements similar to those in fiction, and a close reading can illuminate the books' word choices and the way such choices help make their case.

There are a number of ways English language arts teachers can introduce nonfiction into their classes. While having students read a novel, for example, teachers can assign them biographies of the author to help students understand the world in which the book was written. Other essays and nonfiction can help students understand literature. For example, Colette Bennett, a high school English teacher in Litchfield, Connecticut, has students read Joseph Campbell's *The Hero's Journey,* a book that describes the way writers throughout history have portrayed heroes, in order to prepare for *King Lear.*[23]

Students might also benefit from information about the setting of a novel, particularly if the setting is unfamiliar. By providing some background information about a novel, teachers can engage students in the story before they read it. Ariel Sacks, an eighth-grade teacher in Brooklyn, has students read articles about Indian reservations to help them understand Sherman Alexie's *Absolutely True Diary of a Part-Time Indian,* which takes place on a reservation in Washington State.[24] Sacks also notes that teachers can offer informational materials to students to help them extend their learning beyond the novels they are reading. A discussion about *When You Reach Me,* by Rebecca Stead, which features time travel, led students in her class to read scientific articles about the concept. This additional reading can also help students meet the standards for research; in grade five, for example, students are expected to conduct short research projects that use several sources to build knowledge through investigation of different aspects of a topic.

More Reading, More Books

How can schools accomplish this shift and expand the nonfiction that students are expected to read? Carol Jago, a former president of the National

Council of Teachers of English, says bluntly that students will have to read a lot more than they do now—especially at home. But she notes that students have time to read; they choose to use it in other ways. Citing the 2010 Kaiser Family Media Study, Jago points out that young people aged eight to eighteen spend seven and a half hours a day engaged in electronic media: playing video games, watching television, and social networking. "These are the same students who tell their teachers they don't have time to read," she says. "Children have time. Unfortunately, like Bartleby, they choose not to."[25]

Schools will also have to beef up their libraries and buy new basal readers to build up their nonfiction collections. In a report on the PBS *NewsHour* in 2012, correspondent John Merrow noted that this might be expensive. "Newark schools have been using their basal series for eight years," he said. "But now, with the Common Core's emphasis on nonfiction, some schools will need to buy new editions, or at least complementary books to keep up with the new standards. That's great for the publishing companies, not such good news for schools with tight budgets."[26]

But textbooks are not the only resources available to teachers. By using articles and books connected to a text, as teachers are doing with books like *Absolutely True Diary of a Part-Time Indian,* teachers can provide additional opportunities for students to read without incurring substantial expenses.

CHAPTER

7

Prove It

According to Gerald Graff, a professor of English and education at the University of Illinois, Chicago, the university is an "argument culture." In order to succeed in college, students must be able to engage in arguments—to muster facts to support positions, make cogent points using evidence in speaking and writing, and be prepared to defend positions when challenged. Unfortunately, Graff contends, few high school students are prepared for these tasks; by his estimate, only 20 percent of incoming freshman are capable of conducting the kinds of arguments necessary to succeed in college.

These abilities are critical not only for college but also for the world students will encounter once they graduate. As Joseph M. Williams and Lawrence McEnerney of the University of Chicago writing program put it:

> For four years, you are asked to read, do research, gather data, analyze it, think about it, and then communicate it to readers in a form . . . which enables them to assess it and use it. You are asked to do this not because we expect you all to become professional scholars, but because in just about any profession you pursue, you will do research, think about what you find, make decisions about complex matters, and then explain those decisions—usually in writing—to others who have a stake in your decisions being sound ones. In an Age of Information, what most professionals do is research, think, and make arguments.[1]

The Common Core State Standards reflect this view and expect all students to demonstrate the ability to argue from evidence, in reading, writing, and speaking and listening. The standards make clear that it is not enough to have an opinion; the opinion should be backed up by evidence from a text, and students should be able to read a text closely to glean the necessary evidence.

This expectation is not typical in much classroom practice, according to most observers. Students generally have few opportunities to seek and use evidence, and fewer still to use that evidence to make persuasive arguments. Yet it is precisely these abilities that will be in demand when students graduate from high school and enter college or the workplace.

Critical Thinking

Surveys of college professors show consistently that one of the most important abilities students need to succeed in higher education is *critical thinking*—the ability to analyze information and evidence. Yet, these surveys find, this is one area where incoming students appear to fall short.[2]

Some indication of high school students' inability to analyze evidence comes from the Programme for International Student Assessment (PISA), a test of fifteen-year-olds administered in about sixty countries. In the 2009 PISA, U.S. students performed at about the international average in reading literacy, or about seventeenth among industrialized nations—roughly the same level as Sweden, Germany, and France. However, the U.S. students performed at varying levels on different tasks in the assessment. On tasks requiring students to access and retrieve information—to find, select, and collect information from a text—U.S. students ranked twentieth in the world, more or less in line with their overall standing. Similarly, on tasks asking students to integrate and interpret, or to understand the relations between different parts of a text, U.S. students ranked nineteenth internationally. On tasks requiring students to reflect and evaluate, on the other hand, American fifteen-year-olds performed relatively well. On these tasks, which ask students to draw on their own experience and knowledge to make judgments about a text, U.S. students ranked tenth in the world.[3]

These results suggest that students are relatively skillful at relating texts to their lives, but less so at drawing evidence from the text to support inferences. That is, students are relatively weak at thinking critically about a text. But as Daniel Willingham, a cognitive scientist at the University of Virginia, points out, critical thinking by itself is meaningless; readers need to think critically *about content.* That is, readers must have sufficient understanding of the content a text conveys in order to analyze it.[4]

Close Reading

Finding evidence in a text to support a position takes a particular type of reading, and not all reading is geared toward that purpose. People read books and articles in different ways, depending on the purpose for which they are reading. To get a sense of the main idea, a reader can skim the text and get the gist of what the author is saying. To find specific information, a reader can skip throughout a text to locate the desired facts.

However, a full understanding of a text requires *close reading.* As the term implies, close reading involves a careful examination of a text to focus on the words used, the author's techniques, and the meaning that is evoked. According to the novelist Francine Prose, close reading is how children begin to comprehend texts: "We all begin as close readers. Even before we learn to read, the process of being read aloud to, and of listening, is one in which we are taking in one word after another, one phrase at a time, in which we are paying attention to whatever each word or phrase is transmitting. Word by word is how we learn to hear and then read, which seems only fitting, because that is how the books we are reading were written in the first place."[5]

The focus on the text was the emphasis of much literary criticism in the twentieth century. The idea was that all of the meaning of a text resided within the pages of the text itself, and that the job of the reader was to discern that meaning. More recently, researchers have expanded their view of reading to examine the role of the reader and the reader's response to the text. In that view, a text has only the potential for meaning; the meaning comes about when a reader constructs meaning from it, based on what he or she already knows.[6]

In addition, educators have also come to believe that the reader's own experiences are essential for engaging students in reading. Maja Wilson, who teaches literacy instruction at the University of Maine, and Thomas Newkirk, a professor of English at the University of New Hampshire, say the laserlike focus on what lies within the four corners of the text is "unnatural and probably impossible." They ask readers of their essay, "Have you stayed within 'the text itself'? Have you cordoned off preconceptions, biases, prior reading, and associations until you finish and comprehend this text? Have you bracketed your own views about standards, reading, and what goes on in classrooms so that you can get our message? Or do words like 'standards' and 'reading' invoke your own teaching, learning, and reading histories? Could you suppress this invocation even if you wanted to?"[7]

In many cases, however, efforts to bring the reader in have swung too far. Textbooks and tests often contain questions that students can answer without having read the text at all. For example, teachers at a 2012 workshop in Baltimore examined a textbook that included a narrative poem entitled "When Charlie McButton Lost Power," which was about a boy who finds he cannot use his electronic gadgets during a power outage. Questions at the end of the poem included "What has happened during a bad storm you experienced?" and "How do you feel when you can't do your favorite things?"[8] While such questions might make the poem relevant to some students, they do little to ensure that students are able to comprehend it. Moreover, the focus on students' lives and experiences outside of the text could expose inequities, because more-advantaged students may have had more exposure to experiences outside of class than less-advantaged students. Emphasizing evidence from the text itself levels the playing field.

The National Assessment of Educational Progress provides some data to show that students are weak in their ability to use evidence from a text to demonstrate their understanding of it. On the eighth-grade reading assessment in 2011, for example, students were asked to read a passage on the women's suffrage movement and evaluate the author's choice of words in writing the passage. Student responses were rated on a four-level scale: extensive, essential, partial, or unsatisfactory. Students whose responses were rated "essential" supported an evaluation with one reference from the article. Those rated "partial" provided a general opinion or explained what the language meant. Thirty-six percent of students provided responses rated

essential or above, while 32 percent were rated partial, and 22 percent were unsatisfactory (10 percent did not provide a response).[9]

The Standards' Emphasis on Evidence

The Common Core State Standards make explicit in several places the emphasis on the use of evidence. In an introduction that defines what students who are ready for college and careers know and can do, the document states that such students "value evidence": "Students cite specific evidence when offering an oral or written interpretation of a text. They use relevant evidence when supporting their own points in writing and speaking, making their reasoning clear to the reader or listener, and they constructively evaluate others' use of evidence."[10]

The first "anchor standards"—the standards for career and college readiness that are common for all grades—for reading and writing underline this emphasis. The first anchor reading standard states: "Read closely to determine what the text says explicitly and to make logical inferences from it; cite specific textual evidence when writing or speaking to support conclusions drawn from the text."[11] The first anchor writing standard states: "Write arguments to support claims in an analysis of substantive topics or texts, using valid reasoning and relevant and sufficient evidence." The ninth anchor writing standard states: "Draw evidence from literary and informational text to support analysis, reflection, and research."[12]

In reading, students as early as kindergarten are expected to be able to ask and answer key questions about a text. In grade five, students are expected to "quote accurately from a text when explaining what the text says explicitly and when drawing inferences from the text" (5.RI.1). By middle school, students are expected to be able to cite textual evidence to support an analysis of what a text says and inferences from a text. By grade twelve, students should also be able to determine what a text leaves uncertain.

In writing, students in primary grades should be able to write about a text and cite opinions about it. By grade four, however, students should be able to "provide reasons that are supported by facts and details" (4.W.1.b). By middle school, students should be able to write arguments to support claims with clear reasons and relevant evidence. Such evidence, by grade seven, should include "accurate, credible sources," and the writing should acknowledge alternate or opposing claims (7.W.1.b). By grade twelve, students should be able to develop both claims and counterclaims thoroughly, using the most relevant evidence for each while pointing out the strengths and limitations of both. The conclusion should follow from and support the argument.

The writing standards also include standards for research. Each of these standards emphasizes the use of evidence to support conclusions. The anchor standards state:

7. Conduct short as well as more sustained research projects based on focused questions, demonstrating understanding of the subject under investigation.
8. Gather relevant information from multiple print and digital sources, assess the credibility and accuracy of each source, and integrate the information while avoiding plagiarism.
9. Draw evidence from literary or informational texts to support analysis, reflection, and research.

The speaking and listening standards also require students to attend to and use evidence. In fifth grade, for example, students should be able to "review the key ideas expressed and draw conclusions in light of information and knowledge gained from the discussions" (5.SL.1.d). By grade seven, students should be able to "analyze the main ideas and supporting details presented in diverse media and formats . . . and explain how the ideas clarify a topic, text, or issue under study" (7.SL.2). By grades nine and ten, students should also be able to "present information, findings, and supporting evidence" (9–10.SL.4).

The End of Prereading?

The reading standards, and early interpretations of them, left the impression among some teachers that the Common Core was calling for the elimination of the time-honored practice of prereading. Under that practice, teachers introduce a text by providing background on it to ensure that students can approach the text with sufficient knowledge of the information and vocabulary to be able to read and understand it.

Some of the controversy stemmed from the "publishers' criteria" for the standards, which two lead writers of the English language arts standards, David Coleman and Susan Pimentel, wrote to provide guidance for textbook publishers in preparing materials for teachers based on the standards. The original version of the publishers' criteria stated that "text should be central in instruction," and that publishers should be "extremely sparing in offering activities that are not text-based."[13] Although the authors made clear that they were not suggesting that prereading be banned, they also stated that in many cases, prereading activities had gotten out of hand, and that teachers devoted more time to prereading than to the texts themselves. As a result, students gained information on the prereading activities, not on the evidence from the text itself.[14]

While acknowledging this problem, other educators pointed out that prereading is necessary, particularly for students who may lack the background knowledge necessary to understand a text, and for English language learners who need support in reading English. Providing students with background knowledge and vocabulary is essential to ensure that students can comprehend a text.

A 2012 report by the Aspen Institute attempted to guide teachers through the rhetorical battle. The report noted that background knowledge is essential for comprehension, and said teachers need to know their students well to determine how much background knowledge they have. But, it adds, teachers need to distinguish between the background knowledge necessary to understand a text and the knowledge that the text itself conveys. That is, teachers should not preempt the text with prereading activities, as the publishers' criteria suggests. As the Aspen report states, "previewing the content of a text undermines the value of a Close Reading exercise."[15] If teachers feel students cannot read the text independently to gain information from it, either the text is not appropriate for the students or students are not ready for close reading.

Some teachers have found that they are able to provide students with sufficient background knowledge if they reverse the order and have students read the text, or part of it, first, and then provide them with additional information to fill in gaps. For example, Christiana Stevenson, a teacher at Arsenal Technical High School in Indianapolis, says she has students read Dr. Martin Luther King Jr.'s "Letter from Birmingham Jail" without any preparation. Then, when they start asking questions, she supplies them with information on civil disobedience and the incidents that led to the document. Similarly, Doug Lemov, the managing director of the Uncommon Schools network and author of *Teach Like a Champion,* says that when students read a novel like *Lily's Crossing,* which takes place in New York City during World War II, they take a break after a few chapters to read articles on rationing.[16] In these ways, prereading involves reading.

What Close Reading Looks Like

The Aspen Institute report states that close reading activities may vary, but most share the following characteristics:

- Selection of a brief, high-quality, complex text (including excerpts from longer texts)
- Individual reading of the text
- Group reading aloud
- Text-based questions and discussion that focus on discrete elements of the text
- Discussion among students
- Writing about the text

The idea of having students read the text both individually and as a group is important so that students familiarize themselves both with the language in the text and the information it conveys. Multiple readings help students develop fluency, and also reinforce their knowledge and understanding of a text. Kaycee Eckhardt, a high school teacher in Louisiana, records texts onto a disk so that English language learners can listen to them at home as well as in class.

Text-based questions are critical. As Douglas Fisher and Nancy Frey note, these questions are not intended to have students simply recall facts from the text; rather, they are aimed at probing students' understanding.[17] But there is a range of the kinds of questions that could be asked. Some focus on parts of the text, while others address the text as a whole. Examples of the latter include questions of general understanding; for instance, in a close reading of the Lewis Carroll poem *Jabberwocky,* a teacher might ask, "What is the progress of the hero?" Students would need to turn to the text to describe what happened.

Similarly, questions about the author's purpose involve drawing on the whole text. Students should be able to use evidence to explain what the author was trying to convey and how the way the text was constructed—for example, how an author contrasts the point of view of different characters—served the author's aims.

Questions that involve specific parts of the text probe students' understanding of key details, vocabulary, and text structure. For these questions, a teacher might ask students about specific word choices—for example, "stroll," "amble," "saunter," "meander"—and how each choice alters the tone and meaning of the text. Students can also be asked to draw inferences from specific portions of the text. Using the *Jabberwocky* example, a teacher might ask, "How did the narrator know the Jabberwock was dead?"

The purpose of text-based questions is not solely to elicit literal facts from the text. Questions that ask students to find literal facts in the text can also be used to help them draw inferences from it. For example, in a lesson on a book called *The Wonders of Nature,* a teacher asks a class of second graders to find in the book facts about where trapdoor spiders live. The teacher can then use that information to help the students draw inferences about its protective mechanisms and ways to find food.

Assessment Questions

The assessments being developed to measure student performance against the Common Core State Standards are expected to ask students to draw on evidence to justify their answers. Prototype assessment items and tasks released in the summer of 2012 show what students will be expected to do.

For example, one sample seventh-grade task released by the Partnership for Assessment of Readiness for College and Careers (PARCC) asks students to read three articles about Amelia Earhart, and then asks them to write an essay that analyzes the strength of the arguments about Earhart's bravery in two of the texts, using evidence from the texts to support the conclusions. A separate task, for tenth graders, asks students to use what they have learned from reading "Daedalus and Icarus" by Ovid and "To a Friend Whose Work Has Come to Triumph" by Anne Sexton and write an essay to describe how Icarus's flying is portrayed differently in the two texts. Students are expected to "develop your essay by providing textual evidence from both texts."

The PARCC assessment also asks students to cite examples from the text when responding to questions about specific parts of a text. For example, a sixth-grade task asks students to read a story entitled *Julie of the Wolves,* by Jean C. George. One question asks students to choose a word that best describes Miyax (a main character of the story), using evidence from the text. The question then asks students to find sentences in the passage that support their answer.

Similarly, the sample tasks released by the Smarter Balanced Assessment Consortium expect students to use evidence to justify their answers. One item, for example, asks students to read a story called "Grandma Ruth," about a girl who learns something about her grandmother, who was named for Babe Ruth. Students are asked, "What does Naomi learn about Grandma Ruth. *Use details from the text to support your answer*" (emphasis added).

Writing with Evidence

George Hillocks Jr., a professor emeritus of English at the University of Chicago, notes that argument—writing with evidence—differs from persuasive writing, the kind most often taught in school. Persuasion is aimed at convincing readers of a point, and involves the use of the most favorable evidence and appeals to emotion. Argument, by contrast, "is mainly about logical appeals and involves claims, evidence, warrants, backing, and rebuttals."[18]

As an example of an argument, consider the letter on the League of Nations in figure 7.1. That letter was written by an eighth-grade student after

FIGURE 7.1

We Need the League

Great people of North Dakota,

I, Senator McCumber, [an actual Senator from 1919 in the League of Nations debate], have just participated in a debate regarding whether or not America should sign the Treaty of Versailles, and in doing so, join the League of Nations. The League of Nations is a unified group of nations dedicated to the preservation of peace. The League is designed to deal with international issues, adjudicating differences between countries instead of them going directly to combat.

Now, in the interests of the great state of North Dakota, I voted in favor of the treaty with no reservations. We need a fair treaty to prevent future wars as horrible as the Great War was. After the war, the central powers composed the Treaty of Versailles to create the League of Nations in an attempt to ward off future conflicts. We cannot have another was as horrible as this one. I believe, because of that, that we need a fair treaty, equal to all its members, that will restrict the use of new weapons, and prevent future wars from breaking out.

First, the Treaty and the League will control the use of new weapons. As stated in Article VII, "One of its (the League's) jobs will be to come up with a plan for reducing the number of weapons around the world (arms reduction)." This means that the League will be in charge of weapons issues. This will cause heavily armed countries to demilitarize and make it less possible for war to break out. This is good because heavily armed countries generally end up using those arms in some way.

Another reason why I believe we need to sign the Treaty with no reservations is we need a treaty that is fair to all its members. Reservations [proposed by the League's opponents] would give America too much power within the League, thus allowing America to bend the rules of the League to suit its own will. This would cause unrest in the League, possibly causing America to make enemies. This could lead to another war. The treaty should be as fair as possible.

Yet another reason why I voted for America to sign the treaty is the fact it would prevent future wars from breaking out. The way the League is designed, it would give plenty of time for the League to settle the countries' differences with a fair and equal compromise. If war were to break out, the

(*continued*)

council members in the League would all help in defending each other, thus ending the war as quickly as possible with as few deaths as possible. The treaty would prevent war from happening or end the fighting as quickly as possible.

Some people say that we shouldn't join the League because we would be intervening in foreign affairs, that it would cause another war. How can you not intervene when 8 million people died in the last war? How can you stand there with a clear conscience when you know you could have prevented all that carnage from ever happening? The League will help countries settle their differences with plenty of time to talk it over. Six months for the countries to listen to the council's advice, and after that another three months before they can mobilize. If we join the League, we will keep anything like the Great War from happening again.

In conclusion, the Treaty of Versailles needs to be signed so the League will be put into effect. The League of Nations will prevent war from breaking out, restrict weapons development and militarism, and keep us from the horrors of another Great War.

Thank you.

Source: Vermont Writing Collaborative, South Strafford, Vermont, 2013

a four-week lesson on World War I, in which students used a variety of sources such as videos, maps, and texts, including primary sources, to examine various aspects of the war. At the end of the unit, students took part in a mock senatorial debate on the League of Nations, and then each student wrote a letter to constituents explaining his vote.

This letter does not merely assert an opinion. Rather, it introduces a claim ("We need a fair treaty to prevent future wars as horrible as the Great War was"), organizes reasons and evidence for the claim ("The Treaty and the League will control . . . ," "We need a treaty that is fair . . . ," "It would prevent future wars . . ."), and supports the claim with relevant evidence. The conclusion follows from the claim.

T. J. Hanify, a teacher at the International School in Bellevue, Washington, explained a lesson he has developed to introduce ninth- and tenth-grade students to writing arguments for a segment on the Teaching Channel. Hanify has students read and discuss "Letter from Birmingham Jail," focusing specifically on the way Dr. King makes a case not only to the clergymen to whom the letter was addressed, but to the nation as a whole as well. Hanify then asks students to choose a contemporary incident they have studied, such as the Arab Spring, to consider how Dr. King's ideas are relevant today. He then asks them to write a blog post making an argument, backed with evidence from research, defending the right to challenge unjust laws. Students will then critique one another's blog posts.[19]

The trick is to find topics that both excite students and require them to search for evidence to make sound arguments. Students must also be encouraged to use formats that are engaging. The contemporary parallels to the Dr. King essay represent one way to provide relevance; the mock Senate debate in the World War I project is one way to make the assignment engaging.

Research

The emphasis in the Common Core State Standards on writing arguments is part of a larger emphasis on research. As the Standards document notes, research skills are infused throughout the document, rather than included as a separate strand. This reflects the fact that students need to be able to conduct research to answer questions and solve problems in order to be prepared for college, workplace training, and life in a technological society, the document states.

To underscore that emphasis, both of the consortia developing assessments to measure student performance against the Common Core Standards are expected to include in their assessments tasks that ask students to conduct research. For example, PARCC plans to include a "research simulation" task in which students analyze an informational topic presented through articles or multimedia sources. Students must synthesize information from the sources and write two analytical essays about the topic. Similarly, the Smarter Balanced Assessment Consortium plans to include a performance task that asks students to write several short essays based on multiple texts and videos.

The emphasis on research is likely to heighten the role of school librarians, who can help students find materials to provide evidence to support their claims. As the president of the American Association of School Librarians put it, librarians can help students broaden their search for sources beyond a quick online search. "Students have a false sense of security that they can find anything online, but that's mostly quick facts. They don't know how to ask good, researchable questions, assess information critically. So much of the core is based in inquiry, and that is what librarians do on a daily basis. It speaks our language."[20]

CHAPTER

8

Up the Staircase

TEXT COMPLEXITY

Stephen Colbert had some fun in 2012 with a study that found that members of Congress speak at a tenth-grade level. "America's leaders are speaking like high school sophomores," he said on his June 4 program, "a silent language of angry glares at the dinner table, between text messages."

The study, conducted by the Sunlight Foundation—a Washington, D.C.–based organization dedicated to government transparency—used a commonly applied formula for measuring text complexity known as the Flesch-Kincaid readability test, which looks at vocabulary and sentence length. It found that congressional speeches were at the 10.6 grade level, or about the midpoint of tenth grade. In 2005 a similar study found congressional speeches at the 11.5 grade level. By contrast, the report noted, the U.S. Constitution is written at a 17.8 grade level and the Gettysburg Address at the 11.2 grade level.[1]

Studies with measures like these have shown that the kinds of materials young people read in college and the workplace have remained steady or increased slightly over the past few decades. To read college textbooks and office memos, students graduating from high school should be able to read texts that are at least as complex as the Gettysburg Address.

However, there is evidence that the level of complexity of texts used in high schools has declined over time, so that students on the verge of graduation are reading texts that are less challenging than congressional speeches. The gap between what students are reading and the level of materials they need to be able to comprehend is widening.

The Common Core State Standards aim to close that gap. Citing evidence showing that students' ability to read and comprehend texts at the level they will encounter in college and the workplace is the most important factor in their readiness for postsecondary success, the Standards call for students to be able to read increasingly complex texts. Meeting this standard—and eliminating the gap between high school and postsecondary reading requirements—will require teachers to make judgments about the materials students will read across the grade levels and to develop and apply techniques to enable students who might be behind their grade level in reading ability to understand the texts they will need to read.

Why Text Complexity?

An influential 2006 study by ACT, the college admissions testing organization, identified the factors that were associated with readiness for college. The study found that students who earned the "benchmark" score on the ACT reading test (21 out of 35) have a high probability of success in first-year college courses. According to ACT, that means that such students have a 75 percent chance of earning a grade of C or better or a 50 percent chance of earning a B or better in reading-dependent courses like psychology or U.S. history. Only 51 percent of the students who took the ACT in 2005 reached that benchmark, the study found.

But in addition to reporting the overall findings, the ACT report also examined the factors associated with meeting the benchmark scores. Specifically, the study looked at student performance on different skills measured in the test to see what distinguished those who reached the benchmark from those who did not. Comprehension level—whether students could understand at a literal level or make inferences—did not differentiate students, nor did students' ability to understand textual elements, like the main idea or generalizations and conclusions. What differentiated students was the complexity of texts students could understand. The study divided the reading passages on the test into three types: uncomplicated, more challenging, and complex. Students who answered questions correctly on the more challenging texts did slightly better on the test than those who correctly answered questions only on the uncomplicated texts. However, students who correctly answered questions on the complex texts did substantially better on the test than other students—they scored as many as ten points higher. The pattern held for males and females, all racial and ethnic groups, and all income levels. As the report concludes, "students who can master the skills necessary to read and understand complex texts are more likely to be ready than those who cannot."[2]

Based on this criterion, how ready are high school seniors for college? There are substantial gaps. Studies have found that the complexity of college textbooks has increased since 1962, as has the complexity of scientific journals, which are increasingly used in college classes. The complexity of workplace materials has remained higher than the twelfth-grade level, although there are variations. The level of complexity of newspapers has remained steady since 1963.[3] Moreover, students in college and the workplace are expected to read independently and are accountable for what they read.

Studies of high school textbooks, meanwhile, found that the level of complexity has declined since 1963. Twelfth-grade literature texts published after 1963 are less complex than the *seventh*-grade texts published prior to 1963. And the complexity of texts currently used in grades nine through twelve (except for science textbooks) varies only slightly, and is indistinguishable from the texts used in grades seven and eight.[4] The gap between high school texts and college texts is the equivalent of the difference between fourth and eighth grade texts on the National Assessment of Educational Progress (NAEP).[5]

Some educators claim that the gap has been exacerbated by the practice of many teachers to pitch the books they assign to the perceived reading levels of their students—using texts that are not too easy or too hard, but "just right." In that way, teachers allow students to read books that might challenge them a little without frustrating them. However, some educators argue, such practices do a disservice to students by denying them opportunities to read books that will lead them to levels they will encounter in colleges and the workplace.[6]

Measuring Complexity

Bertha A. Lively and Sidney L. Pressey created the first method for analyzing text complexity (the Lively-Pressey Method) nearly a century ago, and a number of researchers have developed similar measures since then. (These include Rudolf Flesch, author of the best-selling *Why Johnny Can't Read* and co-creator of the method the Sunlight Foundation used to analyze congressional speeches.) In part, this work was supported by the U.S. military, which wanted to ensure that technical manuals could be read and understood by soldiers and sailors.

Over time, publishers used these so-called readability formulas to create texts, such as basal readers, by controlling vocabulary so that students at a particular reading level could understand it. Beginning in the 1980s, though, reading educators began to argue that students should read authentic texts like those they would encounter outside of schools, and educators used the formulas to determine the readability of commercially available books and articles. The formulas generally measure text complexity quantitatively using two dimensions: vocabulary and syntax. They are based on the idea that texts containing a lot of words unfamiliar to students and long, complicated sentences are more difficult to understand than texts using common words and shorter sentences.

One commonly used measure of text complexity, known as a Lexile measure, assesses both the level of complexity of a text (the Lexile text measure) and a student's reading ability (the Lexile reader measure), and places them on the same scale. In that way, teachers can match a text to a student's ability. MetaMetrics, the North Carolina firm that developed Lexile measures, uses a combination of word frequency and sentence length to determine the complexity of reading passages. Students are assigned a reader measure based on their comprehension of those passages. Using that information, MetaMetrics has created a tool, known as Find a Book, that enables parents, librarians, and teachers to identify books matched to children's reading levels as measured on the Lexile scale. The tool is used in fifteen states; in many cases, the information accompanies children's state test results.

While the mathematical formulas provide useful information about text complexity, there are significant limitations, and their results need to be interpreted with care. Although they can provide important information about the vocabulary and syntax students are reading, they are not precise. Specifically, the text-complexity formulas can understate the complexity of narrative fiction. Because many narratives include a heavy use of dialogue, with few infrequently used words and short sentences, they appear from the formulas to be easier than they are. One commonly cited example is Hemingway's *The Old Man and the Sea,* in which the author's relatively simple prose makes the book appear deceptively easy. Consider the book's opening sentence: "He was an old man who fished alone in a skiff in the Gulf Stream and he had gone eighty-four days now without taking a fish." While this sentence is fairly long and includes the possibly unfamiliar word "skiff," it is typical of Hemingway's style of using one-syllable words and few dependent clauses, which makes it appear relatively simple. Yet the metaphors and difficult ideas conveyed in the book make *The Old Man and the Sea* more appropriate for older students.

To take another example, both *Bat Loves the Night,* an illustrated children's book about bats by Nicola Davies, and Mildred D. Taylor's *Roll of Thunder, Hear My Cry,* a popular novel about racial issues in Mississippi that is usually assigned in upper elementary school, have the same Lexile score. That is because the use of dialogue in the novel makes it appear that the syntax is relatively easy, while the ideas are challenging for young readers.

In addition to possibly understating the complexity of narrative fiction, text-complexity formulas can also overstate the difficulty of some informational texts. That is because many such texts use relatively unfamiliar words that are specific to their subject. For example, *Bat Loves the Night* includes a number of rarely used words to describe bats, such as *roost* and *batlings,* which drive up its complexity score. The use of relatively uncommon words is typical of informational texts, because words are not distributed evenly in texts; a phenomenon known as Zipf's Law shows that, in all languages, including English, a handful of words occur frequently, while the vast majority are relatively rare.[7] But in context, such words are generally understandable, even by young children.

Despite these concerns, a study conducted after the release of the Common Core State Standards found that commonly used text-complexity formulas predicted the appropriate grade level of various texts fairly accurately. There were some variations, however; the measures did better with informational texts than with narrative texts, and better with lower grades than with higher grades. But overall the quantitative measures provided a good approximation of the texts' complexity.[8]

What the Standards Say

The English language arts "anchor" Standard 10 for reading—one of the standards for college and career readiness that are common for all grades—places text complexity at the center. It states: "Read and comprehend complex literary and informational texts independently and proficiently." The grade-by-grade standards state that students should be able to read texts that are appropriate for each grade-band level (i.e., 2–3, 4–5, 6–8, 9–10, and 11–College and Career Readiness). Students might need additional support to read texts at the high end of the grade band, the document notes.

To determine text complexity, the Standards document lays out a three-part model using *qualitative measures,* which include aspects of texts best measured by a human reader, such as levels of meaning and purpose; *quantitative measures,* which include aspects of text complexity, such as word length and frequency and sentence length, that cannot be measured easily by human readers; and *reader and task considerations,* which include variables such as student motivation and knowledge and the tasks students are expected to complete with the texts.

Qualitative Measures

Qualitative measures are intended to complement quantitative measures and take into account the factors, mentioned earlier, that make the quantitative measures imprecise, such as the reliance on short sentences in dialogue in narrative fiction and the frequent and repeated use of unfamiliar words in informational texts. In applying qualitative measures, teachers are expected to use their judgment and professional experience to make determinations about where in the grade band the text fits, or whether it belongs in a different grade band. In the Standards document the authors identify four factors that should be included in qualitative measures of text complexity:

- *Levels of meaning or purpose.* Texts with a single level of meaning are easier to read than those with multiple levels, such as satire. Informational texts with implicit purposes are more difficult than those with an explicit purpose.
- *Structure.* The complexity of a text's structure can make it more difficult to read. Narrative texts that shift back and forth in time are more complex than those with a straightforward chronological structure. The use of graphics also affects the complexity of a text; those with simple graphics are easier to read than those with more obscure graphics.
- *Language conventionality and clarity.* A text with clear, conventional language is easier to read than one that relies on irony or unfamiliar language, including jargon and academic language.
- *Knowledge demands.* Texts that require students to draw on background knowledge that is implicit are more difficult than those that do not assume such background knowledge.

Quantitative Measures

Quantitative measures are those that use algorithms to identify the complexity of a text, usually based on word length and frequency and sentence length. The Standards document cites several examples, including the Flesch-Kincaid grade-level test (the measure used to identify the complexity of congressional speeches); the Dale-Chall Readability Formula, which uses word frequency rather than word length; the Lexile Framework for Reading, which, as mentioned above, measures text levels as well as student reading ability based on test performance; and Coh-Metrix, a measure developed at the University of Memphis that aims to assess the cohesiveness of a text, or how a text hangs together. Subsequent documents by the standards writers have identified additional measures.

Reader and Task Considerations

These considerations are important for determining the instructional strategies for using a text, such as the amount of scaffolding and background knowledge required. The document notes that teacher judgment is essential to determine what the reader brings to the text and what the reader will be required to do with it. For example, it notes, a reader who lacks extensive background knowledge about the topic of a text might require some additional materials and support. Cognitive capabilities, knowledge, motivation, and experience are all factors that should be considered. At the same time, teachers must determine whether the text should be skimmed or read closely, and whether it is intended to add to students' knowledge or to help them solve a particular problem.

Examples of Text Complexity

As an example of the three-part model, Appendix A of the English language arts standards includes an analysis of an excerpt from the *Narrative of the Life of Frederick Douglass*. According to the quantitative measures, this book is in the grade six through eight band. The book employs a complex syntax and many obscure words. However, it uses a straightforward storylike structure and draws connections between words. Qualitatively, the book draws on multiple levels of meaning, including an explicit call to end slavery and more implicit discussions of the author's life. Its structure is simple, but it includes some passages that could appear to be digressions. Its language is clear, though it uses some archaic phrases. And its themes are "moderately sophisticated," and background knowledge about slavery is helpful. (Considerations of readers and task should be determined locally, depending on the classroom.) In sum, the document concludes that the

Narrative is appropriate for grades six through eight, especially at the high end of that range.

To take another example, the Standards document considers John Steinbeck's *The Grapes of Wrath.* Quantitative analyses place that book in the grade two to three range. The Coh-Metrix method finds that its syntax is relatively uncomplicated, the story structure is straightforward, and the author uses familiar words. Qualitative analyses, however, show that the book is much more complex than the quantitative analyses indicate. There are multiple levels of meaning, including metaphorical and philosophical, as well as literal. The dialect is challenging for many readers. And the themes are sophisticated and may be foreign to many readers. For those reasons, the book is more suitable for early high school, grades nine to ten. While the book is often assigned at those grade levels, these measures make clear the level of complexity that students should be expected to read and comprehend. (As with the Douglass *Narrative,* considerations of readers and tasks are unique to each classroom.)

Measuring Complexity in the Classroom

Ensuring that students are capable of reading appropriately complex texts implies, first, that teachers can make judgments and determine appropriate levels of complexity. Traditionally, publishers have done a lot of the work for teachers by assigning reading levels to books. But the Standards imply that teachers—and librarians—need to take a more active role in applying the three-part formula outlined in the Standards to determine what books their students should be able to read and comprehend and how these books should be taught.

Since the Standards have been released, several education organizations have developed tools to help teachers make those judgments. The Kansas Department of Education, for example, developed a rubric to help teachers evaluate the qualitative complexity of the texts they assign. The rubric guides teachers through the various qualitative aspects of text complexity—meaning, text structure, language features, and knowledge demands—and helps teachers determine if a particular text is more or less complex based on those aspects. For example, for literary text, a slightly complex text would have one level of meaning; the theme is obvious and revealed early in the text. A very complex text would have several layers of meaning that are difficult to interpret; the theme is implicit or subtle.

Similarly, for knowledge demands, a slightly complex text would require everyday content knowledge, with experiences common to a typical reader, while a more complex text would require extensive, perhaps specialized content knowledge, with experiences different from most readers.

For informational text, the rubric guides teachers through an analysis of text structure, language features, and knowledge demands. Instead of meaning, though, the rubric focuses on the purpose of a given text. In a slightly complex text, the purpose is explicitly stated and clear and concrete; in a very complex text, the purpose is subtle, implied, and difficult to determine.

For an example of the use of the rubric, consider the John Knowles's novel *A Separate Peace*. By quantitative measures the book falls in the grade six through eight band. But there are multiple levels of meaning, the language is challenging, and the knowledge demands—themes of war, jealousy, rivalry, and growing up—are complex. For these reasons, the analysis concludes, *A Separate Peace* is appropriate for students in grades nine and ten.

Similarly, the Text Project, an organization created by Elfrieda H. Hiebert, a researcher at the University of California, Santa Cruz, has developed a four-part process for teachers to analyze the complexity of texts for their classrooms, and has created professional development modules for teachers to guide them through the process. The four steps are:

1. *Gather quantitative information.* Although the overall levels of the quantitative indices are important, two components of the indices—mean log word frequency and mean sentence length—are particularly important for determining the complexity of a text. Teachers and literacy coaches can acquire those data fairly easily.
2. *Compare with benchmark texts.* Educators working with the Text Project have developed a list of "benchmark" texts for each grade level to indicate representative texts that illustrate a particular developmental level. These texts include: for first grade, *Green Eggs and Ham;* for

the end of second grade, *The Bears on Hemlock Mountain;* for the end of third grade, *Beezus and Ramona;* for fourth grade, *The Black Stallion;* and for fifth grade, *The Light in the Forest.* Some, but not all, of the books on the benchmark list were included in the suggested text list in Appendix B of the Common Core State Standards.

3. *Analyze qualitative features that make a text easy or hard.* The Text Project has developed a five-stage rubric for each of the features of a text that affect complexity: levels of meaning/purpose, structure, language conventions and clarity, and knowledge demands. For example, a book at Stage 1 in structure follows the typical structure of its genre (e.g., simple narrative). A text at Stage 3 includes less common genres, such as autobiography. A text at Stage 5 uses traits specific to a content area or unique chronologies or perspectives.
4. *Identify the strengths/needs of readers and the tasks and contexts of classrooms.* Using the developmental stages of reading (prereading, decoding, fluency, reading for learning new content, reading for increasing content knowledge, reading for multiple viewpoints, and construction and reconstruction), teachers should match a text to students' needs and the tasks they are expected to perform with the text. For example, the project's Web site states, "For second graders still at the decoding stage, Henry and Mudge may be too challenging for independent reading but entirely appropriate for a teacher-led lesson on words with two syllables."[9]

Struggling Students

One concern that has arisen about the Standards' requirement for text complexity is what to do for struggling students. In many classrooms, students read well below grade level, and teachers fear that requiring these students—who struggle to read books low on the staircase—will become lost with books that are appropriate for their grade. In that case, teachers say, students might reject reading altogether.

Researchers say the solution for struggling students is not to give up on the idea of text complexity and to try instead to reach struggling students where they are. There is little evidence that students will catch up and be able to read appropriately complex books independently. Rather, some suggest, the solution for struggling students is to provide them with appropriate support and scaffolding to enable them to read books at the appropriate grade-band level. Thomas DeVere Wolsey, Dana L. Grisham, and Elfrieda H. Hiebert suggest that scaffolding should address three issues: background knowledge, "engagingness," and word recognition. That is, teachers should ensure that students have the content knowledge to be able to understand a text—for example, to know what a "constellation" is to read a book about stars. In addition, teachers should engage students in reading and use texts that foster that engagement; the format and illustrations, content, and language are all factors in engagement. And teachers should ensure that students are able to identify words in the text rapidly and accurately and build their vocabulary to enable them to do so.[10]

However, the Standards do not imply that all the reading students do has to be at the appropriate grade level. Students need to demonstrate that they can read complex texts, but the Standards also state that students need to read "widely and deeply," and in order to do that, students need to read a lot. While students can read some texts that are sufficiently complex for their grade level, they can also read additional texts on their own to acquire the habit of reading and build their vocabulary and background knowledge. These additional texts need not be at their grade level.

English Language Learners

One group for whom the complexity standard might be particularly challenging is English language learners. Students who are new to the language might find it difficult to read complex texts. In addition to the use of unfamiliar words, texts in English often include idioms and background knowledge that might be unfamiliar to young people who are developing their English skills.

Understanding Language, an initiative at the Stanford University Graduate School of Education that is developing teaching materials around the Common Core State Standards for English learners, has developed and is piloting a unit on complex texts for middle school students. The unit, called "Persuasion Across Time and Space: Analyzing and Producing Complex Texts," is designed to address a number of reading, writing, speaking and listening, and language standards. The five lessons in the unit guide students through an analysis of persuasive materials, including historical texts, and ask them to produce a persuasive text themselves. The historical texts include the Gettysburg Address, three speeches that show diverse perspectives—Dr. Martin Luther King Jr.'s "I Have a Dream" speech, Robert Kennedy's speech on the death of Dr. Martin Luther King Jr., and George Wallace's "The Civil Rights Movement: Fraud, Sham, and Hoax"—and Barbara Jordan's "All Together Now."[11]

For each lesson, the unit includes options for teachers, depending on the background knowledge and language skills of students. For example, in the lesson on the Gettysburg Address, teachers of students needing maximal scaffolding might read materials with background information aloud, while pausing for students to write comments. The lesson then includes a close reading of the Address; teachers begin by reading the text aloud, with students following in the text, then by having students read portions of it in small groups. The lesson also includes guiding questions for class discussion.

To meet the needs of English language learners and other struggling students, teachers are slowing down their lessons to ensure that students grasp the language in complex texts and that they are able to comprehend them. Norma Lujan-Quiñones, a first-grade teacher in Albuquerque, New Mexico, built a lesson around the story of the Little Red Hen that extended for two weeks, far longer than the two days she previously spent teaching that story. The additional time enabled her to go over the vocabulary—to make sure that students understood the words "sleep," "nap," and "snooze"—and to discuss the meaning.[12] In that way, the "fewer" standards in the Common Core State Standards serve the "higher" goal.

CHAPTER

9

Elevating Discussion

The focus of English language arts instruction in schools has long been on the first two Rs—readin' and writin'. The earliest schools were aimed at enabling children to be able to read the Bible, and reformers in the nineteenth century, like Horace Mann, developed the idea of common schools as a way of enabling young people to be able to read and write to participate in democracy effectively.

Yet while literacy with print is essential, oral language abilities—speaking and listening—play an important role in the development of literacy and are important skills in and of themselves. It almost goes without saying that humans existed for thousands of years without written language, and some of the stories now contained in books, such as Aesop's fables and *The Iliad* and *The Odyssey,* were originally passed along orally. Humans have always needed to speak and listen effectively. Moreover, children are not born knowing how to read, and their earliest exposure to language and texts comes from listening and speaking. Oral communication remains central to children's language development well into their school years.

In addition to helping develop children's literacy abilities, speaking and listening also remain important skills throughout children's school careers, and into college and the workplace. College professors and employers rate speaking and listening abilities high on their list of competencies necessary for success, but find that students who graduate from high school often lack these critical abilities.[1] For these reasons, the Common Core State Standards include standards for speaking and listening. This represents a significant departure from previous state standards. Although states had included expectations for oral language, these tended to take a back seat to reading and writing and were rarely assessed. The Common Core puts these abilities on an equal footing with text-based abilities.

Language Development

As any parent knows, children acquire their first exposure to words and books when parents read to them. These activities help bond parents and children, and there is considerable evidence that they help develop children's literacy abilities. Children whose parents read to them daily perform much better on reading assessments than those whose parents read to them less frequently.[2]

The reasons for this connection are fairly complex. For one thing, many children's books rely on rhyming, which helps introduce children to phonemic awareness. The rhymes reinforce the idea that words are made up of components—phonemes—and that different words might have common phonemes. In addition, books and songs like the Alphabet Song help children learn letters and their sounds.

Second, reading aloud to children develops their vocabulary and background knowledge, a critical factor in reading ability. In one well-known study conducted in the 1980s, researchers Betty Hart and Todd Risley followed a large group of children from birth to age three and found that parents from different socioeconomic groups showed widely different patterns in talking and reading to their children. By age three, they found, the vocabulary of children from professional families was twice as large as that of children from families on welfare; in fact, the vocabulary of children from professional families was larger than that of the *parents* of families on welfare.[3]

Third, reading aloud helps children develop comprehension abilities. Listening and reading are both receptive abilities, and children need to apply the same cognitive processes while listening to stories that they use while reading them. They synthesize ideas and make inferences, and draw on their background knowledge to gain understanding. Researchers have found that listening comprehension and reading comprehension are highly correlated until middle school, when reading comprehension tends to exceed listening comprehension.[4]

Moreover, the ability to listen and read effectively is necessary for students to write and speak well. Speaking and writing are expressive abilities which require the knowledge of words and syntax; listening and reading provide this knowledge. Therefore, listening and speaking are essential for students' writing abilities as well.

Oral language is particularly critical for students whose first language is not English. English has many graphical features that are not present in other languages, even those with similar roots—for example, the "ph" in words like "phonics." Enabling children to become familiar with words before they encounter them on the page is necessary for their reading development.

Oral Communication

While listening and speaking are important for the development of reading and writing abilities, they are also vital skills for college and the workplace. And there is considerable evidence that students currently lack the skills necessary to succeed in higher education and on the job. One survey of 1,815 college professors confirmed the importance of speaking and listening. The survey found that the overwhelming majority of professors surveyed—1,518—considered speaking and listening relevant to their courses, and that they considered these abilities relevant to 79 percent of all courses, and to 85 percent of English language arts courses. These responses were higher than for reading and writing, though lower than for language, or writing conventions.[5]

In addition, the survey found, 78 percent of professors said that the ability to initiate and participate effectively in collaborative discussions was important, and 82 percent rated highly the ability to present information, findings, and supporting evidence in such a way that listeners can follow the line of reasoning.

Yet by students' own reckoning, high schools failed to prepare them for the speaking and listening abilities they needed to demonstrate in college. In one survey, 45 percent of high school graduates said they had gaps in their oral communications skills, more than any other ability; 12 percent said the gaps were large. Among graduates who went into the workplace, 46 percent said there were gaps in their oral communications skills, and 15 percent said the gaps were large. Employers generally agreed with the graduates' self-assessment. A third of employers said they were dissatisfied with the oral communications skills of high school graduates they hired.[6]

Few Opportunities for Speaking and Listening

One reason students might not be developing oral communications skills is that students tend to have few opportunities for speaking and listening in classrooms. In most classrooms, teachers do most of the talking, and when students have a chance to speak, it is usually to respond to a teacher's direct question. This pattern is particularly true in classrooms with low-achieving students.[7]

The traditional pattern of classroom discourse also does little to develop students' abilities to communicate effectively. In many cases, the teacher initiates a question, a student responds, and the teacher evaluates the response. Consider a typical example, from a seventh-grade classroom:

> Teacher: What did the Sumerians use to control the Twin Rivers?
> Student: Levees?
> Teacher: Right.[8]

As Fisher, Frey, and Rothenberg state, this approach is problematic for several reasons:

> First, in a classroom where we want students to talk—to practice and apply their developing knowledge of English—only one student has an opportunity to talk, and, as we see in this example, that talk does not require the use of even one complete sentence, let alone extended discourse. In a classroom where we want students to analyze, synthesize, and evaluate, neither does this type of interchange require them to engage in critical thinking. Instead, they may become frustrated as they struggle to "guess what's in the teacher's head" or become disengaged as they listen to the "popcorn" pattern of teacher ques-

tion, student response, teacher question, student response, and so on. Last, in a classroom where assessment guides instruction, with each question the teacher learns that one student knows the answer but can make no determination regarding the understanding of the other 29 students in the classroom.[9]

By contrast, discussions in which students have opportunities to present information and arguments orally and evaluate the arguments of their peers (and the teacher), while rare, can help students develop not only speaking and listening skills but also the ability to think critically and creatively.

Learning Listening and Speaking

Researchers' understanding of how students learn listening and speaking has evolved over the past few decades, much as it has in other subject areas. Traditionally, listening was understood as the mastery of discrete skills, such as identifying words. More recently, cognitive research has emphasized the importance of prior knowledge and schema, or the ability to create a pattern of thought, and has focused on comprehension and interpretation. The role of the listener is critical.

According to Jack C. Richards, an applied linguist who teaches in Singapore and New Zealand,[10] researchers speak of two ways of approaching listening—"bottom-up processing" and "top-down processing"—and say that schools should teach both. In bottom-up processing, children comprehend oral language by taking apart what was spoken and making sense of it. For example, consider the sentence "The guy I sat next to on the bus this morning on the way to work was telling me he runs a Thai restaurant in Chinatown." To comprehend that sentence, a listener would have to break down the components into chunks—"the guy I sat next to," "on the bus," "this morning on the way to work," and so forth—in order to understand who was speaking, where and when the action took place, and what was conveyed. All that is necessary to understand the sentence is in the sentence itself.

Top-down processing, by contrast, draws on background knowledge to fill in gaps in oral language. The sentence "I heard there was a big earthquake in China last night" does not contain all the information necessary to understand it. A listener needs to know what a "big" earthquake is, what an earthquake can do, and where China is, in order to assess what the speaker is saying. Such knowledge affects how the listener interprets any subsequent sentences.

Speaking is somewhat more complicated, because speech has several different purposes. Richards describes three types of speech: talk as interaction (e.g., conversations between friends and colleagues); talk as transaction (e.g., telephone calls to receive flight information, purchases in shops); and talk as performance (e.g., classroom presentations, speeches). Each of these would be evaluated in different ways.[11]

What the Standards Say

The Common Core State Standards for English language arts include two broad standards for speaking and listening: Comprehension and Collaboration, and Presentation of Knowledge and Ideas. Although these headings appear to correspond to "listening" and "speaking," respectively, they both contain aspects of each. The standards are designed to integrate speaking and listening, and to link speaking and listening to the rest of the English language arts standards.

For example, the Comprehension and Collaboration standards are active, rather than passive, standards. They state:

1. Prepare for and participate effectively in a range of conversations and collaborations with diverse partners, building on others' ideas and expressing their own clearly and persuasively.
2. Integrate and evaluate information presented in diverse media and formats, including visually, quantitatively, and orally.
3. Evaluate a speaker's point of view, reasoning, and use of evidence and rhetoric.

Thus the standards expect students not only to listen to other speakers and assess their arguments, but also to participate actively in discussions and express their own points of view. Students should expect to speak as well as listen.

Similarly, the Presentation of Knowledge and Ideas standards expect students to be active participants in discussions, and to listen attentively and speak with their peers. The standards state:

4. Present information, findings, and supporting evidence such that listeners can follow the line of reasoning and the organization, development, and style are appropriate to task, purpose, and audience.
5. Make strategic use of digital media and visual displays of data to express information and enhance understanding of presentations.
6. Adapt speech to a variety of contexts and communicative tasks, demonstrating command of formal English when indicated or appropriate.

That is, students should make presentations in ways that respect their audience and communicate in ways that the audience can understand. In that way, the communication is interactive; the listeners help shape the presentation.

The Standards document notes further that students should have opportunities to participate in a range of speaking and listening situations. These should be "rich, structured conversations" around important content in a variety of domains, and should include whole-class discussions as well as one-on-one conversations. The document also notes that electronic means of communication have broadened the opportunities students have for discussion, and suggests that classrooms take advantage of those opportunities.

The standards make clear that these expectations should begin as early as kindergarten. In that grade, students are expected to participate in conversations with partners about "kindergarten topics and texts"; ask and answer questions; describe familiar people, places, things, and events; add drawings or visual displays to presentations; and express thoughts audibly and clearly.

By grades eleven and twelve, students should be able to integrate multiple sources of information; evaluate a speaker's point of view; present information, findings, and supporting evidence such that listeners can follow the line of reasoning; make strategic use of digital media; and adapt speech to a variety of contexts and tasks.

The reading and writing standards complement these standards by asking students to demonstrate their understanding of texts and to express their ideas persuasively and convincingly. These tasks can—and should—be done through thinking and listening. For example, a reading standard for grade eight states: "Evaluate the advantages and disadvantages of using different mediums (e.g., print or digital text, video, multimedia) to present a particular topic or idea" (RI. 8.7). To accomplish this standard, students must have opportunities to make multimedia presentations. Thus, providing students with such opportunities can enable them to meet both this reading standard and the speaking and listening standards.

Similarly, the writing standards for grades six through twelve state that students should "develop and strengthen writing" through guidance and support from peers and adults. This standard thus implies that students should have opportunities to present their writing in class and receive verbal feedback.

The Standards in Practice

The first step in implementing the speaking and listening standards is providing students with opportunities for oral presentations. As noted earlier, classrooms tend to be dominated by teacher talk, with teachers speaking as much as two-thirds of the time, and student speech limited to responding to teachers' questions. Developing oral communications skills requires more extensive speaking time. This does not mean that teachers give the class over to students for free-form conversation. Rather, teachers implementing the standards have found ways to facilitate structured discussions among students that enable them to present information effectively and evaluate the presentations of their peers.

The Institute for Learning at the University of Pittsburgh's Learning Research and Development Center refers to these types of discussions as "accountable talk." As the Institute states on its website:

> Talking with others about ideas and work is fundamental to learning. But not all talk sustains learning. For classroom talk to promote learning it must be accountable to appropriate knowledge, and to rigorous thinking. *Accountable*

> *Talk* seriously responds to and further develops what others in the group have said. It puts forth and demands knowledge that is accurate and relevant to the issue under discussion. *Accountable Talk* practices use evidence appropriate to the discipline (e.g., proofs in mathematics, data from investigations in science, textual details in literature, documentary sources in history) and follows established norms of good reasoning. Teachers should intentionally create the norms and skills of *Accountable Talk* practices in their classrooms.[12]

One way teachers are doing this is by tying speaking and listening to other English language arts standards, such as reading and writing. For example, teachers are engaging students in argumentation not just through writing but also through speeches. In this way teachers can address the standards for the use of evidence (see chapter 7) as well as the standards for speaking and listening.

One example of this approach was presented on a series of Teaching Channel videos by Julie Manley, an eighth-grade teacher at Chinook Middle School in Bellevue, Washington. In a three-and-a-half-week unit, Manley's students develop and deliver speeches designed to provide persuasive arguments. They begin by writing what they know about argumentation. They then look at published speeches and analyze the elements of argumentation in them. Based on that analysis, the students write "be sure to's"—things they must be sure to do or avoid doing in their own speeches.

Then the students present their speeches. To ensure that the rest of the class listens effectively, Manley has prepared guidelines for them. Students must identify the speakers' claims and the evidence they use for them. They then meet in small groups to evaluate the presentations and provide a critique. They also write a list of "be sure to's" based on these critiques for their speeches.

The Institute for Learning has developed curriculum materials for teachers to implement similar units of study. In one unit, students in ninth and tenth grade conduct a close reading of three speeches focused on the issue of racial equality: Dr. Martin Luther King Jr.'s "I Have a Dream" speech, President Bill Clinton's "Remarks to the Convocation of the Church of God in Christ," and President George W. Bush's speech to the 2000 NAACP convention, "Ending Racial Inequality." Based on their analysis of each speech, students compare the argumentation in the speeches. As one option, students can prepare presentations. In small groups, students review the reasoning, evidence, and methods used by each of the speakers to propose solutions to racial inequality. They then prepare five-minute speeches to present to the class. As they present their speeches, their classmates consider the strength of their presentation. This unit thus combines standards for speaking and listening with standards for reading, since it requires students to use text-based evidence to support their conclusions (see chapter 7).

Socratic Seminars

Another way teachers have introduced speaking and listening into classrooms is through the use of Socratic seminars. Socratic seminars are not new; the late educator Mortimer J. Adler proposed the idea thirty years ago in his book *The Paideia Proposal.*[13] Adler, the former editor of the Great Books series, proposed organizing classrooms into seminars around open-ended questions about classic texts. Students discuss these works by answering questions that ask them to interpret them, using evidence from the texts to form their arguments. One popular variation of the approach is to organize the class into two groups: one to discuss the text and the other to evaluate their peers' discussion.

Christina Procter, a tenth-grade teacher at the High School for Arts, Imagination, and Inquiry in New York City, uses Socratic seminars to develop students' abilities to support claims and refute counterclaims—a key element of the Common Core State Standards for reading and writing—as well as to develop their oral language competencies. In a video on the Teaching Channel, Procter describes a lesson in which students use *Persepolis,* a graphic novel by the Iranian writer Marjane Satrapi, to debate why governments can be oppressive and why some groups of citizens are oppressed.

At first, Procter has her students work in small groups to brainstorm claims and counterclaims. Students take notes on the discussion. Then each small group sends a representative to the front of the room to begin the debate. "That's the point when the teacher really becomes silent, and that's the beautiful part of the lesson, when students are simply talking," she says.

The debating students use a symbol—in the case on the video, a stuffed squirrel—to ensure that only one person talks at a time and the others listen respectfully. Only the person holding the squirrel can speak, and students must ask for the squirrel to respond. When other students want to enter the debate, they tap their representative on the shoulder and replace her.

To help ensure that students meet standards for using evidence, Procter awards points for making a unique claim, for referring to evidence from the text, and for anticipating and refuting a potential counterclaim. Students note that the format also develops their abilities to speak and listen effectively. One notes the "level and maturity and respect" in the discussion.

Using Technology

Technology offers myriad and different opportunities for classroom lessons to build speaking and listening skills. As the Standards document itself notes, "New technologies have broadened and expanded the role that speaking and listening play in acquiring and sharing knowledge and have tightened their link to other forms of communication. The Internet has accelerated the speed at which connections between speaking, listening, reading, and writing can be made, requiring that students be ready to use these modalities nearly simultaneously. Technology itself is changing quickly, creating a new urgency for students to be adaptable in response to change."[14]

For example, elementary teachers at PS 62 in Queens have students conduct a "talk show" to discuss Chris Van Allsburg, the author of books they are reading. That is, rather than—or in addition to—writing their responses to the text, students present their reactions orally, and are evaluated on their oral presentations.

Technology can also be helpful for English language learners and students with disabilities. Students can speak into microphones and be recorded by computers, rather than speak to an entire class; in that way, classrooms with English language learners can help ensure that such students do not feel intimidated by speaking in front of their peers. Additionally, digital media and other computer-based systems can enable students with disabilities, such as those with visual or auditory impairments, to take part in speaking and listening activities by using voice recognition or closed-captioning and other technologies.[15]

Technology can also help students who are initially reluctant to speak before a group. Students can record their presentations on a computer or on video, which can then be shown to the class. Students can also use Skype or a similar platform to speak to groups outside their class; they can listen to TED Talks and speeches that have been posted on YouTube.

Assessing Speaking and Listening

Both of the consortia that are developing assessments to measure student performance against the Common Core State Standards are planning to develop assessments of speaking and listening. At the time of this writing, these assessments are still in process; it is unclear exactly what they will look like or how they will be administered. But schools and other countries have developed speaking and listening assessments. Although they were not designed to measure the Common Core State Standards, they offer a glimpse into how speaking and listening can be evaluated.

Like the Common Core, England's national curriculum includes expectations for speaking and listening. The curriculum states: "Pupils should be taught in all subjects to express themselves correctly and appropriately and to read accurately and with understanding. Since standard English, spoken and written, is the predominant language in which knowledge and skills are taught and learned, pupils should be taught to recognise and use standard English. In speaking, pupils should be taught to use language precisely and cogently. Pupils should be taught to listen to others, and to respond and build on their ideas and views constructively."

In response to that directive, the Lancaster County Council in 2010 launched an action research project to develop assessments of speaking and listening. The assessments were part of regular classroom units. For example, in one "key stage 1" (age 7) assessment, the teacher read to the class the fantasy story "Whatever Next!" The students were asked to listen to the detail and the descriptions and to imagine the setting. They were then asked to retell the story to a partner, and then to switch places, so the partner retold the story to the first student. Students were rated on a 1 to 4 scale; for example, a Level 3 student will:

- Talk and listen confidently in different situations
- Sequence, explore, and communicate ideas in an organised way
- Show understanding of the main points in a discussion
- Show they have listened carefully through making relevant comments and questions
- In most situations, be able to adapt what they say to meet the needs of the audience/listener
- Vary the use of vocabulary and level of detail
- Start to show awareness of how and when standard English is used
- Show understanding of characters and contexts by changing voices, actions, and movements[16]

Educators in the United States have developed similar assessments. For example, one assessment posted on Share My Lesson, a teacher resource developed by the American Federation of Teachers, assesses high school students' abilities to contribute to a group discussion on the staging of a portion of *A Midsummer Night's Dream*. Students' discussions are rated on a seven-point scale; a student reaches Level 7 by demonstrating the following abilities:

- Confidently matching talk to the demands of different contexts
- Communicating clearly using precise vocabulary
- Making significant contributions which also evaluate others' ideas
- Using Standard English confidently and fluently

With these kinds of practices, teachers' voices will no longer be the only sounds in classrooms.

CHAPTER

10

A Role for Everyone

For decades, educators have argued that reading and writing are not the sole province of English classrooms. Recognizing the vital role of literacy in understanding content in science, history, and other subjects, educators have called for efforts to infuse reading and writing instruction in all subjects. These efforts have often gone by the names Reading Across the Curriculum and Writing Across the Curriculum.

The results of these efforts have been mixed at best. In part, they have failed to gain traction because, at least until recently, there has been little reading and writing instruction—in any subject, including English language arts—beyond third grade. Schools seemed to operate under the assumption that once students mastered the basics of reading and writing, they could use those skills to learn in all subject areas. More recent research has shown that this view is misguided, and that students need instruction in reading and writing throughout their school career, to address the different demands for literacy in the middle and high school grades.[1]

In addition, teachers of science, history, and other subjects seldom saw their role as teaching reading and writing. Although they recognized the importance of literacy in developing content knowledge, teachers tended to view their job as focusing on the content knowledge and skills, rather than in developing literacy skills.

The Common Core State Standards are explicit in identifying the literacy demands of the content areas. The formal name of the English language arts standards is "Common Core State Standards for English Language Arts *and Literacy in History/Social Studies, Science, and Technical Subjects.*" The standards include specific standards for reading and writing in each subject for grades six through twelve. These standards are based on the idea that literacy is learned throughout the curriculum, and that the literacy demands of each subject area are unique.

Implementing these standards will require greater attention to the growing body of research on reading and writing in the disciplines. If successful, it will finally make good on the decades-old promise for reading and writing across the curriculum.

The Challenge of Adolescent Literacy

A solid body of research has shown that early reading ability is a strong predictor of later academic success. According to one review, "A person who is not at least a modestly skilled reader by the end of third grade is unlikely to graduate from high school."[2] In the face of such evidence, policy makers have devoted substantial resources to early-reading programs, with the goal of ensuring that all children learn to read by grade three. Most notably, the federal No Child Left Behind Act included a $1 billion program, known as Reading First, that provided funds to states and districts to develop and expand early-reading initiatives.

These efforts have produced some success; the proportion of fourth graders who attained the proficient level on the National Assessment of Educational Progress rose from 29 percent in 2000 to 34 percent in 2011, while the proportion who scored below the basic level declined from 41 percent to 33 percent during that period.[3] Yet those gains did not persist in the later grades. Reading performance at grades eight and twelve has remained flat since 1998.[4]

Why did the improvement in the early grades fail to generate improvement in middle and high school? One reason is that the efforts in the early grades tended to focus on enabling students to "break the code" and read words; there was less of an emphasis on ensuring that students could comprehend what they read. Evaluations of Reading First, for example, showed that the program had little effect on comprehension.[5] As a result, students did not develop the skills they needed to understand the more complex texts they read as they got older, and reading performance failed to improve.

In addition, many schools paid little attention to reading and writing instruction after grade three. As a brief by the Alliance for Excellent Education put it:

> In many cases, there is a lack of both interest and capacity to teach adolescent literacy skills to our secondary students. Most middle and high school teachers, including English teachers, see themselves as content specialists and have not received training—either in teacher-preparation courses or in professional development offerings—to teach literacy skills within their subject area. To further compound the problem, there is a wide variation with regard to how well, if at all, states are incorporating literacy standards—especially comprehension skills—throughout the content areas, and if these specific standards are being assessed. Therefore, students' chances of benefiting from these skills are totally dependent on their state of residence.[6]

Reading and Writing in the Disciplines

While there has been little attention to reading and writing instruction in secondary schools, there has been even less to literacy instruction across the curriculum. In fact, there is evidence that writing, at least, has declined in subjects other than English. A 2002 study found that eighth graders reported writing a paragraph or more in 46 percent of social studies classes, 32 percent of science classes, and 13 percent of mathematics classes. By 2007, the proportion of social studies classes with writing assignments dipped to 44 percent, and the proportion of science classes with writing assignments dropped to 30 percent. Writing in mathematics stayed stable during that time.[7]

Twelfth graders, meanwhile, reported even less writing; students said they wrote at least a paragraph in 42 percent of social studies classes, 21 percent of science classes, and 8 percent of mathematics classes. (A recent study showed that students write little in English classes as well; 39 percent of twelfth graders reported writing a page or less for English classes a week, with 13 percent saying they wrote nothing.)[8]

Recent research suggests that simply expanding reading and writing instruction across the curriculum can be counterproductive. Literacy is not generic; the skills necessary to analyze historical documents and write essays describing a historical event are different from those required to comprehend and write a scientific journal article. As one recent report put it:

> The ways in which successful students read algebra textbooks (for example, working to translate word problems into an understanding of the problem being posed and a representation of the problem in algebraic terms, then working to arrive at a single, correct mathematical solution) don't apply to reading and interpreting modern poetry (which calls for sustained attention to word choice, tone, the relationship of form to content, narrative voice, the use of metaphor and symbol, and other aspects of language that don't often come into play when studying algebra). And the ways in which students write up chemistry notes (crafting a detailed, impersonal, accurate record of steps taken and reactions observed) may not be helpful when trying to write a history paper or literary analysis.[9]

This point of view suggests that the goal of literacy instruction in the content areas is not to teach reading comprehension or writing as ends in themselves, but rather to enable students to engage in literacy activities that are essential to the content area. That is, teachers need to develop students' abilities to read and write like a historian or scientist so that they can develop their understanding of history and science. And, research shows, these practices improve students' overall reading and writing abilities.[10]

Standards for Literacy in the Content Areas

The Common Core State Standards state explicitly that literacy is fundamental to the content areas, and that the literacy demands of each content area are unique. For example, the document states that in the area of history, "students need to be able to analyze, evaluate, and differentiate primary and secondary sources."[11] In science and technical subjects, meanwhile, students need to be able to comprehend texts with challenging diagrams and data. The document makes clear, however, that these literacy expectations are intended to complement the content expectations for each subject area, not replace them.

The content-area literacy standards are for grades six through twelve only; the standards for the earlier grades are embedded in the reading and writing standards for those grades, the document states. The content-literacy standards are for reading and writing only; there are no separate standards for language or speaking and listening for history, science, and technical subjects.

The standards follow the "anchor" standards in reading and writing. These anchor standards are the expectations for career and college readiness that all students should achieve by the time they graduate from high school. The grade-by-grade standards are intended to lead students to those levels.

In reading, the first anchor standard states that students read closely to determine what the text says and to make inferences from it. The first standard for grade six through eight for literacy in history/social studies states that students should be able to "cite specific textual evidence to support analysis of primary and secondary sources" (6–8.RH.1). By grades nine and ten, students should also "attend to such features as the date and origin of the information" (9–10.RH.1), in order to evaluate the quality and trustworthiness of the evidence. And by grades eleven and twelve, students should be able to connect insights gained from specific details to an understanding of the text as whole.

Similarly, in science and technical studies, students in grades six through eight should be able to cite evidence to support analysis of scientific and technical texts; in grades nine and ten, to attend to precise details of explanations; and in grades eleven and twelve, to attend to the author's emphases or any inconsistencies or gaps.

The writing standards likewise follow the anchor standards for writing—for the most part. The first set of anchor writing standards refer to text types and purposes, and include writing for argument, informative and explanatory writing, and narrative writing. But the literacy standards for history/

social studies and science and technical subjects state that narrative writing is not applicable. Rather, the standards state, narrative writing should be incorporated into the informative and explanatory writing. For example, it states, informative and explanatory writing should include the narration of historical events, scientific procedures, or technical processes.

The standards also state that students should produce clear and coherent writing, using revision and editing and taking advantage of technology; conduct short and more sustained research projects; and write routinely on discipline-specific tasks, purposes, and audiences.

Suggested Readings

In keeping with the Standards' emphasis on ensuring that students are capable of reading and understanding complex texts, an appendix to the Common Core document lists some suggested readings that exemplify the appropriate complexity at various grade levels. In addition to literary works and informational texts in English language arts, the appendix also includes some exemplary informational texts in science, social studies, and technical subjects.

For example, for grades six through eight in history/social science, the appendix suggests the Preamble and First Amendment to the U.S. Constitution; Phillip Isaacson's *A Short Walk Around the Pyramids and Through the World of Art;* Elizabeth Partridge's *This Land Was Made for You and Me: The Life and Songs of Woody Guthrie;* and Russell Freedman's *Freedom Walkers: The Story of the Montgomery Bus Boycott,* among others. In science and technical subjects, the suggested readings include David Macaulay's *Cathedral: The Story of Its Construction;* Ivars Peterson and Nancy Henderson's *Math Trek: Adventures in the Math Zone;* "Elementary Particles," from the *New Book of Popular Science;* and the California Invasive Plant Council's *Invasive Plant Inventory.*

For grades nine and ten, suggested informational texts for history/social science include Dee Brown's *Bury My Heart at Wounded Knee,* Mark Kurlansky's *Cod: A Biography of the Fish That Changed the World,* and Wendy Thompson's *Illustrated Book of Great Composers.* For science, mathematics, and technical subjects, suggested texts include Euclid's *Elements,* Richard Preston's *The Hot Zone: A Terrifying True Story,* and the pamphlet *Recommended Levels of Insulation,* from the U.S. Environmental Protection Agency and the U.S. Department of Energy.

This last title (and the invasive plant manual from grades six–eight) raised some eyebrows among some commentators, who appeared to believe that these technical manuals would push literary works like *The Adventures of Huckleberry Finn* out of the curriculum (see chapter 6). But as the appendix makes clear, these suggested texts are for science and technical subjects, not English language arts. English language arts classes remain safe for Mark Twain.

A Welcome Change

Although some teachers of subjects other than English expressed some reservations about the Standards' requirements for literacy in the content areas, many others embraced the idea as a welcome move. Teachers recognized the importance of reading and writing in their disciplines and sought ways to incorporate literacy into their instruction.

Indeed, a 2010 statement issued by six professional organizations representing teachers in a wide range of disciplines states clearly that literacy instruction is fundamental to disciplinary learning. The statement, entitled "Principles for Learning," was prepared by the Association for Career and Technical Education, the Consortium for School Networking, the National Council for the Social Studies, the National Council of Teachers of English, the National Council of Teachers of Mathematics, and the National Science Teachers Association. Its first principle states that "being literate is at the heart of learning in every subject area." It adds that teacher training, professional development, and scholarly research should enable teachers to help students read and write in their subject area.

The word appears to be getting out. A 2012 survey conducted by the National Science Teachers Association found that two-thirds of the science teachers polled said that they are being asked by their supervisors to spend time on reading in science.[12] For some teachers, the literacy work provides a way to introduce students to some of the fundamental concepts in the discipline. For example, Sara M. Poeppleman, a science teacher at Lewis County High School in Vanceburg, Kentucky, has her high school chemistry students read "$E = mc^2$: The Most Urgent Problem of Our Time," a 1946 article by Albert Einstein in a popular science magazine. That text, along with an article associated with a PBS series about the legacy of the famous equation, explains core content in nuclear chemistry, she says.[13]

At the same time, the use of reading and writing in content areas also makes the content more relevant to students. Teachers can have students write essays about contemporary topics with which they are familiar, while making sure that they demonstrate appropriate scientific and technical concepts. Poeppleman, the Kentucky science teacher, did this by having students write essays about radiation in airport x-ray scanners. Mason Kuhn, a fourth-grade teacher at Shell Rock Elementary School in Iowa, had students write a science-themed book for second graders.

Infusing literacy into the content areas can also make possible collaboration across disciplines. History teachers teaching about the civil rights movement can have students read Dr. Martin Luther King Jr.'s "Letter from Birmingham Jail" to explore the significance of that document for the movement at the time, while those in English classes can read it closely to understand its power as a rhetorical document.

Some educators caution, however, that such connections should be made judiciously. Christine A. Roye, a professor of science education at Shippensburg University, told *Education Week* that not every topic is ripe for connection. "With science and literacy, don't force the issue. There will be natural places where it will be a great match," she said.[14]

Literacy Design Collaborative

To assist teachers in developing tasks for student reading and writing in the content areas, the Literacy Design Collaborative, an initiative funded by the Bill and Melinda Gates Foundation, has created "template tasks," or shells of student assignments, that teachers can fill in to present to students. These template tasks are organized around the three genres of writing in the Common Core State Standards in English language arts: argumentation, information/explanatory, and narrative.

The tasks, which are generic and applicable to a range of grade levels, are designed to probe a range of student knowledge, from definition and description to synthesis and analysis, from problem/solution to cause-and-effect. For example, a definition task template for informational texts asks students:

> After researching __________ (informational texts) on ____________ (content), write a ________ (report or substitute) that defines ________ (term or concept) and explains __________ (content). Support your discussion with evidence from your research.

An example from science is:

> After researching scientific articles on magnetism, write a report that defines "magnetism" and explains its role in the planetary system.

One task template for cause-effect in informational text is:

> After researching _________ (informational texts) on ___________ (content), write a _________ (report or substitute) that examines causes of __________ (content) and explains effects of ________ (content). What conclusions or implications can you draw? Support your discussion with evidence from your research.

An example of such a task from social studies is:

> After researching historical sources on America's love of the automobile, write a report that examines causes of the expansion of the automobile in America and explains effects on America's culture. What conclusions or implications can you draw? Support your discussion with evidence from your research.

Teachers in Kentucky who piloted the tasks said they were skeptical of them at first, but grew to like them when they saw the effects on their students' work. Beth Fallbush, a social studies teacher at Scott High School in Taylor Mill, Kentucky, told *Education Week* that it was "foreign at first" to be teaching reading and writing in social studies classes. "We had that mentality that you're not an English teacher, you're a social studies teacher, so that needs to be taken care of in another class," she said. "When I first started doing it, it definitely did take time away from my content, and I didn't like it. But now that I'm in the second year, I see that I am teaching the content, just doing it through the writing assignments. The social studies teachers talk about it; we all see our students writing better, and we can see from their open-ended and constructed responses that they are understanding the concepts better."[15]

Students, likewise, initially found the tasks daunting, but also grew to appreciate them. Dylan Rohrer, a senior at Dixie Heights High School in Fort Mitchell, Kentucky, wrote a short essay arguing that juveniles should be tried as adults, and found it challenging. "It looked so innocent, just that little paragraph, but man, it was way harder than it looked," he said. "We spent like two weeks researching stuff, and we had to justify everything we said. I'm a pretty good writer, and I can usually just get by, writing, you know, whatever. But I actually had to think through things. When I was done, I considered it an accomplishment. It was interesting to be challenged in school."[16]

Assessment Tasks

The assessments being developed by the two state consortia to measure student performance on the Common Core State Standards (see chapter 1) can help facilitate the move toward literacy in the content areas. These assessments are expected to include materials from history, science, and technical subjects and ask students to analyze them. Schools that use assessments to help guide instructional decisions will likely shift toward reading and writing in all subjects.

A sample seventh-grade task released in 2012 by the Partnership for Assessment of Readiness for College and Careers (PARCC), for example, asks students to read three documents about Amelia Earhart: a biography, an article about the discovery of her plane, and an article about her life and disappearance. After reading the biography, students are asked to write an essay summarizing the challenges she faced in her life. Then, after reading the article about the discovery, students are asked to analyze claims made by the article and find evidence to support them. Finally, students are asked to write an essay about Earhart's bravery, using evidence from at least two of the texts.

Similarly, a sample item released by the Smarter Balanced Assessment Consortium asks students to watch a video about how astronauts exercise in space. The assessment asks students to answer a multiple-choice question to get a literal meaning from the video, then to write an essay explaining why exercising in space is important, using evidence from the video.

Science Standards

The effort to integrate literacy into content areas could receive a boost with the adoption and implementation of Next Generation Science Standards (NGSS), a set of standards for that subject that were developed under the auspices of Achieve. The standards, released in 2013, are based on a framework developed by the National Research Council, which focuses on three dimensions of science: core ideas in life science, physical science, earth/space science, and engineering; cross-cutting concepts, such as patterns, cause and effect, and systems; and scientific and engineering practices, such as developing and using models and carrying out investigations.[17]

The scientific and engineering practices, in particular, are closely aligned to the Common Core State Standards for English language arts. One practice calls for constructing explanations (for science) and designing solutions (for engineering); a second calls for engaging in argument from evidence; and a third calls for obtaining, evaluating, and communicating evidence. To make these links explicit, the standards document shows how specific science standards correspond to specific English language arts standards from the Common Core State Standards.

In an essay on the language demands of the NGSS, Helen Quinn, Okhee Lee, and Guadalupe Valdés note that "language is essential to successfully engage in any of these practices and all of the practices provide language learning opportunities."[18] However, they note, such opportunities also pose challenges for English language learners. Such students need support to develop reading comprehension competency, particularly if their ESL instruction focused primarily on decoding skills. At the same time, English language learners need support to comprehend scientific texts, which differ from texts in other genres and from spoken language. Yet, they add, "it is not a service to language learners to 'protect' them from the demands of subject area reading."[19]

The same could be said for all students.

CHAPTER

11

The Road Ahead

IMPLEMENTING THE COMMON CORE STATE STANDARDS

In a book entitled *Standards Deviation,*[1] James Spillane, a professor of learning and organizational change at Northwestern University, analyzed what happened in nine Michigan school districts in the early 1990s after the state introduced new standards for mathematics. The standards were intended to lead to substantial changes in classroom practice and, ultimately, higher levels of student performance. But as the cleverly worded title of his book shows, teachers interpreted the standards in widely varied ways. Some saw them as substantial changes in practice and made corresponding adjustments to their instruction, while others viewed them in a relatively superficial way, making few changes. There was little change in student achievement.

Spillane offers several reasons for the varied reactions to the standards. Because of a dispute between the governor and state education department, there was a reduction in staffing at the state level, which curtailed the state's ability to provide resources and assistance to schools. Districts, too, differed in the level and kind of support they provided to schools and teachers. And the state test was in significant ways misaligned to the standards; to the extent teachers focused on the test, they missed important aspects of the standards. In the end, Spillane saw the communication between the state and schools as akin to the children's game of telephone, in which the standards were whispered from the state capitol to classrooms, only to create a muddled message at the end of the line.

Spillane's story of Michigan mathematics standards in the early 1990s highlights many of the challenges states now face as they put in place plans to implement the Common Core State Standards. As the previous chapters have shown, the Standards in many ways call for substantial changes in classroom practice. To make those changes real, states, districts, and private organizations need to develop and make available new assessments, curriculum materials, instructional resources, and professional development to ensure that teachers understand the Standards and their implications for classroom practice, and that they have the support needed to make the necessary changes in their instruction. If there is a "standards deviation," the impact of the Standards on classroom practice and, ultimately, student learning, will be muted.

But despite the challenges, states and districts are moving ahead with implementation efforts. And there are a number of factors that make it more likely than in the 1990s that these efforts will succeed. For example, the availability of technology makes possible a much more widespread dissemination of resources and professional development. In this smartphone era, the game of telephone might be a thing of the past.

A Status Check

A January 2012 report by the Center on Education Policy (CEP), based on a survey of officials from thirty-seven states that have adopted the Common Core State Standards, found that all surveyed states had developed plans for implementing the Standards, and all planned to have them fully in place by 2014, the year that assessments tied to the Common Core Standards are expected to be administered.[2] Specifically, the survey found that all states planned to adopt or revise assessments used in the interim and to revise curriculum materials aligned to the Common Core Standards; develop and disseminate materials for professional development; and carry out statewide professional development activities. Most, but not all, states planned to align teacher preparation programs to the Common Core Standards and to modify or create educator evaluation systems that hold educators accountable for mastery of the Standards.

Far fewer states were aligning higher education requirements with the Common Core, however. Only sixteen states said they were aligning undergraduate admissions requirements with the Standards by making sure that entrance criteria reflected the knowledge and skills embodied in the Standards, and the same number were aligning entry-level coursework with the Standards by ensuring that the courses did not duplicate what students were expected to have learned in high school.

Significantly, states said that funding was a challenge to implementation. Twenty-one states said that finding adequate resources to carry out implementation activities was a "major" challenge, while eight states—primarily states that won federal grants under the Race to the Top program, which provided twelve states with a total of $4.35 billion for reform plans—called it a "minor" challenge.

A separate survey conducted jointly by Education First, a consulting firm based in Seattle, and Editorial Projects in Education (EPE), the organization that publishes *Education Week,* showed similar results. All states reported that they had implementation plans, and all but one had fully developed plans to provide professional development for teachers; most had plans to adopt aligned curriculum materials, and to revise teacher-evaluation systems to reflect the standards.[3]

The CEP and Education First–EPE surveys show that states were moving forward in their implementation efforts. But state progress has not been uniform; some states are farther ahead than others. One state that has aggressively pursued implementation is Kentucky, which was the first state to adopt the Standards. (Kentucky adopted the Common Core Standards in February 2010, four months before they were formally released.) The Bluegrass State has undertaken extensive efforts to prepare teachers to work with the new standards, make changes in classroom instruction, and make expectations clear for students.

For example, the Kentucky Department of Education prepared an extensive analysis that compared the Common Core with Kentucky's previous standards, and distributed it widely. Kentucky Educational Television also prepared online units for parents, teachers, and community members to explain the Standards, and the Pritchard Committee, a statewide organization of civic leaders, developed a campaign to explain the Standards and why they matter to parents and community members across the state.

The state department of education also built an online portal called Kentucky's Continuous Instructional Improvement Technology System, which will host lessons, tests, and curriculum materials at the click of a mouse. The system will also include podcasts produced by higher education faculty to help educate teachers about new instructional strategies designed around the Standards.

The state has also engaged its higher education institutions. The Council of Postsecondary Education, the governing body of colleges and universities, is working with the K–12 education system to develop assessments based on the Standards to be used to determine placement in first-year college courses. And colleges of education are redesigning their teacher-preparation program to align them with the expectations of the Standards.

Kentucky also took the controversial step of retooling its state test in 2012 to align with the Common Core Standards. This move raised eyebrows because state officials were well aware that the instructional changes had not all taken root, and that many students were not prepared for the higher standards the test would assess them on. They fully expected that the results would show that far fewer students demonstrated proficiency on the new standards, compared with the number who had reached the proficient level on the previous test.

Indeed, the first results, released in October 2012, showed what appeared to be a sharp drop in performance. In reading, 48 percent of elementary students were proficient, compared with 76 percent the previous year with the old test; the proficiency rate among middle school students dropped from 70 percent to 46.8 percent. In mathematics, the drop was steeper, from 73 to 40.4 percent in elementary school, and from 65 percent to 40.6 percent in middle school.

Other states are also working to prepare teachers and develop materials to support them in implementing the Common Core Standards in the classroom. For example, West Virginia laid out a plan to provide extensive professional development to all its teachers on the Standards. The state held week-long workshops for kindergarten teacher leaders in 2011–2012, and held similar workshops for teacher leaders in grades one, four, five, and nine in 2012–2013, and plans to hold workshops for teacher leaders in the remaining grades in 2013–2014. The leaders are then expected to hold workshops in their home districts; school administrators are also required to attend the workshops. West Virginia is also developing materials for teachers. Teams of teachers met in late 2011 to review the standards and state-adopted curriculum materials and identify gaps. The teachers then developed project-based learning units to fill the gaps and uploaded them onto a state Web portal.

In Maryland, meanwhile, teams of teachers, curriculum specialists, and subject-matter experts used the Common Core State Standards to revise the state's model core curriculum, and they expanded its Online Instructional Toolkit to link the curriculum to lesson plans, instructional materials, and assessment items. The state department of education also formed partnerships with the Maryland Business Roundtable, Maryland Public Television, and the College Board to widen the distribution of digital materials.

Massachusetts is revising its state test, the Massachusetts Comprehensive Assessment System (MCAS), by incorporating topics from the new Standards and dropping topics that are not included in the Standards. At the same time, the state department of education engaged three hundred teachers in a process of developing model curriculum units and performance assessments aligned to the Standards. The plan is to develop a hundred model units by 2014. The units are expected to become part of the state's Teaching and Learning System, which will include tools to monitor student progress, assessments, curriculum units, and videos of classroom practice.

Utah, meanwhile, created the Utah Common Core Academy for more than five thousand teachers and principals to help districts and charter schools redesign curriculum and implement the Standards. The state department of education created several opportunities to follow up on the academies. For example, the department held seminars with secondary teachers to explore assessment.

National and Cross-State Efforts

While the state efforts are under way, national organizations and firms are also engaged in developing materials and preparing educators to revamp instruction and supervision around the Common Core Standards. The fact that the Standards have been adopted by so many states make possible cross-state partnerships that could not have taken place when each state developed its own standards.

The most extensive cross-state effort to implement the Common Core Standards is represented by the two state consortia that are developing the assessments to measure student performance against them (see chapter 1). In 2010, the U.S. Department of Education awarded $330 million to the Partnership for the Assessment of Readiness for College and Careers (PARCC) and the Smarter Balanced Assessment Consortium (SBAC) to develop assessments in English language arts and mathematics for grades three through eight and high school aligned to the Common Core. PARCC currently consists of twenty-two states, and SBAC includes twenty-four states (one state belongs to both). These consortia have proposed ambitious plans to create tests that include performance tasks—for example, asking students to conduct research and write essays to argue a point from the evidence they have found—and to administer their tests online, taking advantage of technology to use items and tasks not possible with paper-and-pencil tests.

In addition to developing the assessments, the two consortia are also supporting states and districts in the implementation of the Common Core Standards. To support these efforts, the U.S. Department of Education awarded each of the consortia an additional $16 million in early 2011.

As part of its supplemental proposal, SBAC said that it would create a digital library of curriculum frameworks, sample instructional units, and formative assessment tools, and that it would involve nearly 2,800 teachers in identifying or creating these tools. The consortium also plans professional development to help teachers understand the assessment system and how to score test items.

Similarly, PARCC also plans to develop instructional and curriculum tools for teachers. The consortium plans to create the Partnership Resource

Center (PRC), an interactive online tool that will include curriculum frameworks and model lessons, as well as test items to use formatively in the classroom. In addition, PARCC will develop an online diagnostic tool that will enable teachers to evaluate the complexity of a particular text. This tool will help teachers identify appropriate materials to enable students to meet the standards for reading increasingly complex texts, a critical component of the Common Core State Standards. The partnership also plans to create an interactive data tool and reports that will help teachers gather and use data on student achievement to support instructional decisions and assist principals in making decisions about professional development needs.

Under its supplemental grant, PARCC will also create "college-readiness tools," including coursework to help students who are not on track toward college readiness at the end of eleventh grade. Like SBAC, PARCC plans to create a digital library of curriculum resources and assessment tools.

Both consortia are taking steps to engage higher education institutions in the implementation of the Standards. The Standards are intended to measure students' readiness for postsecondary education, but they will only have meaning if colleges and universities accept them as measures of readiness. In their proposals, the consortia lined up letters of support from public institutions of higher education in the participating states, which pledged to use them to help place incoming freshman in math and English courses. PARCC received letters of support from 188 institutions; SBAC received support from 162 institutions.

As part of their assessment-development activities, the consortia have been meeting with higher-education representatives to set standards for the assessments. The goal is to ensure that the standard for college readiness matches the expectations of colleges and universities for first-year students.

Other cross-state efforts are under way as well. In one notable effort, a group of universities, community colleges, and school districts in thirty states have formed the Mathematics Teacher Education Partnership to redesign teacher-preparation programs aligned with the Common Core State Standards. Funded in part by the National Science Foundation, the partners include sixty-eight institutions of higher education and eighty-seven school districts.

Private groups are working to develop materials and provide professional development as well. Student Achievement Partners, a New York–based organization founded by two of the lead writers of the Common Core State Standards, David Coleman and Jason Zimba, received an $18 million grant from the GE Foundation to create "immersion institutes" to familiarize teachers with the Standards and to create a storehouse of materials for them to use in their instruction.

Publishers are also moving to develop new materials based on the Standards. One of the largest such efforts is being undertaken by Pearson, a major publisher based in London. With input from members of teams that wrote the Standards, Pearson is creating a series of K–12 curriculum materials that will be delivered completely online, through tablets like the iPad. They will include projects for students to complete, texts and digital materials to support students in conducting their projects, and assessments to check student understanding. The firm has received support for this effort from the Bill and Melinda Gates Foundation; as a condition of this support, some of the materials will be available to all schools free of charge.

Other publishers are likely to follow suit, because the forty-six states that have adopted the Common Core Standards represent a near-national market. To help encourage the development of materials aligned with the Standards, a group of twenty large urban districts that are part of the Council of Great City Schools banded together to press publishers to create materials that match the Standards' expectations. The districts are hoping their leverage can influence the development of better products.

The Funding Challenge

While these efforts at the state and national levels appear promising, states and districts face significant challenges in implementing the Common Core State Standards. Perhaps the biggest is finding the funds for implementation. As noted above, more than half the states identified funding as a "major" implementation challenge.

How much will implementation cost? Two national organizations commissioned research to find out. The Pioneer Institute, a Boston-based organization that has been critical of the Common Core, issued a report in February 2012 stating that implementation would cost states a total of $15.8 billion over seven years.[4] This total included $1.2 billion for new assessments, $5.3 billion for professional development, $2.5 billion for textbooks and instructional materials, and $6.9 billion for technological infrastructure and support. Of the total, the report notes, $10.5 billion were "one-time" costs associated with putting the Standards in place; the rest were ongoing expenses.

A separate report issued by the Thomas B. Fordham Institute, a supporter of the Common Core Standards, addressed what the authors called some of the flaws in the Pioneer analysis and came out with more modest estimates.[5] For one thing, the report notes, many of the activities states will undertake to implement the Standards are things they do regularly—states buy new instructional materials, administer assessments, and conduct professional development every year. A realistic estimate of the cost of implementing the Common Core Standards would examine what states would pay on top of what they already pay for these expenses. In addition, the Fordham report notes, there are many ways to implement the Standards. States can take advantage of technology and open-source materials and save money. A fair analysis would show a range of approaches.

Based on these premises, the Fordham report outlined three scenarios, and estimated the net cost—on top of annual expenses—for each:

- Business as usual, which would mean using hard-copy textbooks, in-person professional development, and paper-and-pencil tests, would cost $8.2 billion
- Bare bones, which would involve open-source materials, online assessments, and online professional development, would cost $-927 million (states would save money)
- Balanced implementation, which would represent a mix of the two, would cost $1.2 billion

The report also notes that states can use the opportunity the Common Core Standards provide to form multi-state collaborations and save money.

Other challenges also loom. While the Common Core State Standards are creating opportunities for the development of new materials and new professional development offerings, not all of these products and services will be truly aligned to the Standards or be of high quality. How can educators make informed decisions about the quality of curriculum materials?

The cross-state partnerships made possible by the Common Core are offering one solution. Three states—Massachusetts, New York, and Rhode Island—have developed a tool to evaluate materials for their alignment to the Standards and their quality. Officials from the states shared this tool with those from a larger group of states in the spring of 2012, and the states plan to pilot the tool with English language arts materials. More activities like this are likely.

Another challenge concerns the assessments that the PARCC and SBAC consortia are developing to measure student performance against the Standards. Because of the importance of tests in state accountability systems, teachers tend to place a greater emphasis on what is tested than what is actually contained in the standards.[6] In the 1990s, many state tests were poorly aligned to state standards, so the influence of standards was reduced, as Spillane's story of Michigan showed.

As they build their assessments, the consortia are working hard to make sure that they reflect what the Common Core State Standards expect. Both consortia work closely with leaders of the teams that drafted the Standards to ensure that their interpretation of the Standards is accurate and that the items and tasks they develop for inclusion on the assessments truly measure what the Standards intend all students to know and be able to do. In addition, both consortia are using a process for developing assessments known as "evidence-centered design" to help ensure that the assessments measure what the Standards intend. Under that process, the consortia begin with claims they want to make about student performance derived from the Standards, determine what evidence they need to make those claims in a valid manner, and then develop items and tasks that will provide that evidence.

However, both consortia also face challenges that could limit their ambitious aims. One challenge is financial. The kinds of assessments both consortia are developing, which rely more heavily than most state tests on open-ended tasks and student writing, are likely to be more expensive than many current state tests. That's because these tasks require humans to score them, as opposed to multiple-choice tests, which can be scanned and scored by machine very cheaply. Yet once the federal funds for developing the assessments dry up—on September 30, 2014—states will be responsible for the costs of administering them. State legislators might be reluctant to increase the amount they spend on student assessments, and the pressure to keep costs down might force the consortia to trim their sails.

A report by the Brookings Institution estimated that states currently spend, on average, $27 per pupil on mathematics and English language arts tests, slightly more than the two consortia estimate for their assessments.[7] However, state spending varies widely, from $13 per pupil in Oregon to $105 per pupil in Hawaii. The report noted that states actually spend considerably more than this total on assessments, including the costs of additional assessments (such as tests in other subject areas) and other expenses, such as state personnel. Total actual spending on assessments, the Brookings report estimated, was $1.7 billion, or $65 per pupil. While that total might seem high, the report noted that it represented just one-fourth of 1 percent of total spending on education.

Nevertheless, states that spend less for tests than the consortia assessments are likely to cost might be leery of increasing spending. Researchers have found ways that these costs could be reduced. First, the Brookings report notes, developing tests as a consortium would reduce costs, since groups of states could spread fixed costs, like the cost of developing and field-testing items, over a much larger student population. The two consortia are likely to reap those cost savings. In addition, a report from the Stanford Center for Opportunity Policy in Education (SCOPE) found that states could reduce costs through the use of technology, as the consortia plan to do.[8] Delivering tests on computers eliminates the costs associated with printing and distributing test materials. In addition, such tests could be scored electronically, reducing the costs associated with gathering teachers to score essays by hand. A competition sponsored by the William and Flora Hewlett Foundation identified promising approaches to computer scoring of essays.

While electronic scoring might reduce costs, it also takes away a big advantage of teacher scoring: the professional development benefit of engaging teachers in an examination of student work against standards. But the SCOPE report also pointed out that these costs could be considered professional development costs, rather than assessment costs, thereby driving down the testing total.

The assessment consortia also face pressure to keep the scope of their assessments manageable. In order to measure the full range of standards in ways that capture what the standards expect (for example, using extended tasks that ask students to conduct research and write essays based on the evidence they find), the assessments could end up taking more classroom time than current state tests do. Some states might blanch at adding time for testing, particularly since many parents and teachers believe that current state tests eat up too much learning time. In response to these concerns, the Smarter Balanced Assessment Consortium agreed to limit the number of performance tasks on its assessment, so that the total amount of testing time would be seven hours in grades three through five, seven and a half in grades six through eight, and eight and a half in grade eleven.[9]

Consortia officials have been working to communicate with policy makers and the public about the length of the assessments to build support. For one thing, they note, the additional time provides more information about student progress on the Standards. Shorter assessments would not be able to measure all of the standards or provide sufficient data on student abilities. In addition, the consortia officials note, extended tasks are a learning experience for students. If students are spending their time conducting research and writing essays, they are engaging in educational activities; this is not time taken away from instruction. Other countries rely heavily on such extended tasks—in many cases, their assessments could take weeks to complete—and there is little sense that these tasks mean "too much testing."

Political Challenges

The concern over public support for new assessments points up a broader political challenge states face in implementing the Common Core State

Standards. Although the Standards won broad approval among educators and public officials and were adopted by nearly all the states, the support was not necessarily widespread in the public at large. A survey conducted by Achieve in 2012 found that 60 percent of voters had heard nothing about the Common Core State Standards, while another 19 percent had heard "not much." However, when provided with a brief description of the Standards, the vast majority of people expressed support for them. More than three-fourths of all voters said they supported the Standards, and 45 percent expressed strong support.[10]

Teachers, meanwhile, were very familiar with the Standards—65 percent had heard a lot about them—and very supportive. The more teachers knew about the Standards, the more likely they were to support them. A survey by the American Federation of Teachers in 2013 found that 75 percent of that union's members supported the Standards, although many teachers feared that they were not prepared to teach them.[11]

Nonetheless, a minority of voters expressed opposition to the Standards, and in several cases this opposition has led to attempts to scuttle or reverse adoption of the Standards. In many cases, this opposition reflects the misimpression that the Common Core State Standards were a federal initiative, sponsored by President Obama. Although the Obama administration supported the effort—and awarded points to states that adopted the Standards in its Race to the Top competition—the initiative was led and managed by the states. But the misimpression remained alive; during the 2012 Republican National Convention, speakers referred to the Common Core Standards as "Obama-Core," a derisive reference to the term used for President Obama's health care law, Obamacare.

Reflecting this view, legislators in several states, such as South Carolina and Utah, proposed bills that would have given state legislatures a vote in standards adoption (the Common Core Standards were adopted for the most part by state boards of education) or would have rescinded the adoptions outright. In South Dakota, a lawmaker went a step further and proposed a bill to prohibit the state from adopting common social studies standards, something that did not exist. All of these efforts have failed as of March 2013. In addition, the American Legislative Exchange Council, an organization of mostly conservative state lawmakers, considered but did not adopt a resolution opposing the Common Core Standards. And in Alabama, the newly elected governor, Robert J. Bentley, asked the state board of education to reconsider its vote to adopt the Standards; that effort was defeated.

Some opposition efforts had partial success. In Utah, the state board of education went ahead with adoption and implementation of the Standards, but it voted to pull the state out of one of the assessment consortia, as did Alabama. And in Indiana, a former teacher named Glenda Ritz in 2012 defeated the incumbent state superintendent of public instruction, Tony Bennett, who had been a strong supporter of the Common Core Standards. Ritz and her backers opposed Bennett on many grounds, including his positions in favor of teacher evaluation and vouchers, but she also attracted some support from conservatives who had opposed his stance on the Standards. The legislature subsequently passed a measure that would "pause" implementation of the Standards.

Although these efforts to block the Standards have failed to stem the tide in their favor, the thin layer of public support for the Standards remains a concern to the initiative's supporters. Without a stronger base of support, states might not be able to muster the political backing necessary to fund the implementation. The level of support is particularly worrisome since more than half of the governorships and state chief positions changed hands after the release of the Standards, meaning that most of the state leaders who presided over the formation of the initiative were no longer in office when it came time to put implementation plans in place.

Supporters of the Common Core Standards have also been concerned about what will happen when the first results are released from the new assessments designed to measure student performance against them. Because these assessments are likely to include some tasks that many students have had little exposure to prior to 2010, and because the expectations for student performance represented by the Standards are considerably higher than in many states' previous standards, the test scores are expected to be lower. As noted above, Kentucky got a first taste of this experience in 2012, when it released scores that were as much as 40 percent lower than the previous year's. Many Standards advocates fear that what appears to be a drop in student performance might convince some policy makers to abandon the effort.

But Kentucky's experience, as well as a similar experience the year before in Tennessee, shows that this scenario might be too gloomy. In both of those states, advocates made a concerted effort to inform the public about the new standards and tests and to make the case that the results don't mean that students are getting worse; rather, that the expectations are higher and more realistic, and that they are putting in place efforts to strengthen student performance in the future. Those messages seemed to be effective.

The True Test

The true test of the Common Core State Standards, and of public support for them, will come over the next few years as states carry through their implementation plans. Will test scores rise over time? Will students be better prepared for college and careers?

Judging by the amount of activity that has taken place since the adoption of the Standards, and that is likely to continue over the next few years, states are making a strong bet that this round of standards-setting will produce better results than the previous round in the 1990s. The level of activity states are engaged in, the possibilities offered by technology and cross-state collaborations, and the extraordinary effort to develop new assessments all suggest that the Common Core State Standards might generate some real changes in classroom instruction. And, they further suggest, these changes will be widespread, and will lead to real improvements in student learning.

States are implementing the Common Core Standards because they are convinced that it is in their best interest, and in the interest of the nation as a whole, for all young people to develop the knowledge and skills the Standards expect students to learn. The first step in making that happen is recognizing what the Standards expect, and how that might be different from what students were expected to learn in the past. The previous chapters have attempted to describe those shifts, and the ways that schools are implementing them. The next step is to make it happen in tens of thousands of schools across the country.

APPENDIX

Resources on the Common Core State Standards

THE STANDARDS

To read the standards themselves, as well as appendixes, background information, and information on state adoption, see the Common Core State Standards Web site, www.corestandards.org.

NEWS ABOUT STANDARDS

The best source of news on the Common Core State Standards and their implementation is Education Week's Curriculum Matters blog, where Catherine Gewertz and Erik Robelen are on top of every development: http://blogs.edweek.org/edweek/curriculum/. In addition, the Thomas B. Fordham Institute's Common Core Watch blog, written by Kathleen Porter-Magee, provides incisive commentary on the Standards and their implementation: http://www.edexcellence.net/commentary/education-gadfly-daily/common-core-watch/.

SUPPORTING ORGANIZATIONS

Organizations supporting the Common Core State Standards have posted a wealth of information on the Standards and their adoption and implementation, including sample tasks, videos, and other information. See Student Achievement Partners, which was formed by the lead writers of the Standards, at www.achievethecore.org; the Illustrative Mathematics Project, created by William McCallum, a lead author of the mathematics standards, at www.illustrativemathematics.org; America Achieves, at http://commoncore.americaachieves.org; the James B. Hunt Jr. Institute for Educational Leadership and Policy, at www.youtube.com/user/TheHuntInstitute; the Text Project, at www.textproject.org; and the Teaching Channel, at www.teachingchannel.org.

ASSESSMENT CONSORTIA

The two consortia of states developing assessments to measure the Common Core State Standards have a wealth of information on their Web sites about their plans and activities. See the Partnership for Assessment of Readiness for College and Careers site (www.parcconline.org) and the Smarter Balanced Assessment Consortium site (http://www.k12.wa.us/SMARTER/).

Notes

Preface

1. Catherine Gewertz, "Teachers Say They Are Unprepared for Common Core," *Education Week* 32, no. 22 (Feb. 27, 2013): 1, 22.

Chapter 1

1. Lauren B. Resnick, "From Aptitude to Effort: A New Foundation for Our Schools," *Daedalus* 124, no. 4 (Fall 1995): 55–62; Marshall S. Smith and Jennifer O'Day, "Systemic School Reform," in *The Politics of Curriculum and Testing: The 1990 Yearbook of the Politics of Education Association,* eds. S. H. Fuhrman and B. Malen (Bristol, PA: Falmer Press, 1991), 233–68.
2. Diane Ravitch, *National Standards in American Education: A Citizen's Guide* (Washington, D.C.: Brookings Institution, 1995).
3. David Coleman and Jason Zimba, *Math and Science Standards That Are Fewer, Clearer, Higher to Raise Achievement at All Levels* (New York and Princeton, NJ: Carnegie Corporation of New York–Institute for Advanced Study Commission on Mathematics and Science Education, 2007).
4. Minnesota adopted the standards in English language arts only.
5. Center on Education Policy, *States' Progress and Challenges in Implementing Common Core State Standards* (Washington, D.C.: CEP, Jan. 2011).
6. Two other consortia are developing assessments for students with severe cognitive disabilities, and two additional consortia are developing assessments of English language proficiency for students whose native language is not English.

Chapter 2

1. William Schmidt, Richard Houang, and Leland Cogan, "A Coherent Curriculum: The Case of Mathematics," *American Educator* 26, no. 2 (Summer 2002): 3.
2. William H. Schmidt, Curtis C. McKnight, Richard T. Houang, Hsing Chi Wang, David E. Wiley, Leland S. Cogan, and Richard G. Wolfe, *Why Schools Matter: A Cross-National Comparison of Curriculum and Learning* (San Francisco: Jossey-Bass, 2001).
3. Robert Rothman, "Benchmarking and Alignment of State Standards and Assessments," in *Redesigning Accountability Systems for Education,* eds. S. H. Fuhrman and R. F. Elmore (New York: Teachers College Press, 2004), 96–114.
4. David Coleman and Jason Zimba, *Math and Science Standards That Are Fewer, Clearer, Higher to Raise Achievement at All Levels* (New York and Princeton, NJ: Carnegie Corporation of New York–Institute for Advanced Study Commission on Mathematics and Science Education, 2007), 4 (emphasis in original).

5. William McCallum, "The Common Core Standards in Mathematics" (paper prepared for the Twelfth International Congress on Mathematical Education, Seoul, Korea, July 8–15, 2012).
6. Coleman and Zimba, *Math and Science Standards.*
7. Ibid, 7.
8. Rick Hess, "Straight Up Conversation: Common Core Guru Jason Zimba," Rick Hess Straight Up (Feb. 11, 2013), http://blogs.edweek.org/edweek/rick_hess_straight_up/2013/02/rhsu_straight_up_conversation_sap_honcho_jason_zimba.html.
9. McCallum, "Common Core Standards in Mathematics," 9.
10. PARCC, *PARCC Model Content Frameworks: Mathematics, Grades 3–11* (Washington, D.C.: Achieve, Oct. 2011), http://www.parcconline.org/mcf/mathematics/appendix-b-starting-points-transition-common-core-state-standards/.
11. PARCC, *PARCC Model Content Frameworks,* 20.

Chapter 3

1. James W. Pellegrino, Naomi Chudowsky, and Robert Glaser, eds., *Knowing What Students Know: The Science and Design of Educational Assessment* (Washington, D.C.: National Academy Press, 2001).
2. Phil Daro, Frederic A. Mosher, and Tom Corcoran, *Learning Trajectories in Mathematics: A Foundation for Standards, Curriculum, Assessment, and Instruction.* CPRE Research Report #RR-68. (Philadelphia: University of Pennsylvania, Consortium for Policy Research in Education, Jan. 2011), 23.
3. Ibid.
4. Pellegrino, Chudowsky, and Glaser, eds., *Knowing What Students Know,* 182.
5. National Research Council, *Common Standards for K–12 Education?: Considering the Evidence. Summary of a Workshop Series* (Washington, D.C.: National Academies Press, 2008), 15.
6. Jerome S. Bruner, "On Learning Mathematics," *The Mathematics Teacher* 53, no. 8 (Dec. 1960): 610–19.
7. Adam Gamoran, "Beyond Curriculum Wars: Content and Understanding in Mathematics," in *The Great Curriculum Debate: How Should We Teach Reading and Math?,* ed. T. Loveless (Washington, D.C.: Brookings Institution Press, 2001), 138.
8. National Governors Association and Council of Chief State School Officers, *Common Core State Standards for Mathematics* (Washington, D.C.: NGA and CCSSO, 2010), 4.
9. Achieve, *Achieving the Common Core: Comparing the Common Core State Standards and Singapore's Mathematics Syllabus* (Washington, D.C.: Achieve, 2010).
10. Personal communication, Jan, 29, 2013.
11. http://ime.math.arizona.edu/progressions/.
12. The Common Core Standards Writing Team, *Progressions for the Common Core State Standards in Mathematics: K–6 Geometry* (Tucson, AZ: University of Arizona, Institute for Mathematics in Education, 2012), 5, http://commoncoretools.files.wordpress.com/2012/06/ccss_progression_g_k6_2012_06_27.pdf.
13. Ohio Department of Education, *Mathematics Model Curriculum* (Columbus, OH: ODE, 2011), 5.
14. NGA and CCSSO, *Common Core State Standards for Mathematics,* 5.

Chapter 4

1. National Council of Teachers of Mathematics, *Curriculum and Evaluation Standards for School Mathematics* (Reston, VA: NCTM, 1989), 3.
2. Alan H. Schoenfeld, "The Math Wars," *Educational Policy* 18, no. 1 (Jan.–Mar. 2004): 268.
3. Quoted in ibid., 273–74.
4. Quoted in David Klein, "A Quarter Century of US 'Math Wars' and Political Partisanship," *BSHM Bulletin* 22, no. 1 (2007): 22–33.
5. Phil Daro, "Math Warriors, Lay Down Your Weapons," *Education Week* 25, no. 23 (Feb. 15, 2006): 34–35.
6. National Governors Association and Council of Chief State School Officers, *Common Core State Standards for Mathematics* (Washington, D.C.: NGA and CCSSO, 2010), 4.
7. Ibid.
8. Barry Garelick, "A New Kind of Math Problem: The Common Core State Standards," *The Atlantic* (Nov. 12, 2012), http://www.theatlantic.com/national/archive/2012/11/a-new-kind-of-problem-the-common-core-math-standards/265444/
9. Hung-Hsi Wu, "Phoenix Rising: Bringing the Common Core Mathematics Standards to Life," *American Educator* 35, no. 3 (Fall 2011): 4 (emphasis in original).
10. Erik W. Robelen, "Big Shifts Ahead for Math Instruction," *Education Week* 31, no. 29 (Apr. 25, 2012): S24, S25, S26, S28, S30.
11. James W. Stigler and James Hiebert, *The Teaching Gap* (New York: The Free Press, 1999).

Chapter 5

1. National Research Council, *A Framework for K–12 Science Education: Practices, Crosscutting Concepts, and Core Ideas* (Washington, D.C.: National Academies Press, 2012), 26.
2. Alan H. Schoenfeld, "The Math Wars," *Educational Policy* 18, no. 1 (Jan.–Mar. 2004): 268.
3. National Council of Teachers of Mathematics, *Principles and Standards for School Mathematics* (Reston, VA: NCTM, 2000), 4.
4. Jeremy Kilpatrick, Jane Swafford, and Bradford Findell, *Adding It Up: Helping Children Learn Mathematics* (Washington, D.C.: National Academies Press, 2001).
5. Stephanie Z. Smith, Marvin E. Smith, and Thomas A. Romberg, "What the NCTM Standards Look Like in One Classroom," *Educational Leadership* 50, no. 8 (May 1993): 4–7.
6. National Center on Education Statistics, *The Nation's Report Card: Mathematics 2011* (Washington, D.C.: U.S. Department of Education), 52.
7. James W. Stigler and James Hiebert, *The Teaching Gap* (New York: The Free Press, 1999), 11–12.
8. Ibid., 11.
9. National Governors Association and Council of Chief State School Officers, *Common Core State Standards for Mathematics* (Washington, D.C.: NGA and CCSSO, 2010), 8.
10. Ibid., 72.
11. Ibid., 73.
12. http://hub.mspnet.org/index.cfm/mspnet_academy_teaching_common_core/.

Chapter 6

1. Brad Phillips, "Teaching with the Lights On," *RE: Philanthropy,* Sept. 29, 2011, http://www.cofinteract.org/rephilanthropy/?p=3399.
2. Arthur N. Applebee, "Stability and Change in the High School Canon," *English Journal* 81, no. 5 (Sept. 1992): 27–32.
3. Arthur N. Applebee, *A Study of High School Literature Anthologies* (Albany, NY: State University of New York, Center for the Study of Literature, 1991).
4. Nell K. Duke, "The Real-World Reading and Writing U.S. Children Need," *Kappan* 91, no. 5 (Feb. 2010): 68–71.
5. J. Hoffman, S. McCarthey, J. Abbott, C. Christian, L. Corman, C. Curry, et al., "So what's new in the new basals? A focus on first grade," *Journal of Reading Behavior* 26 (1994): 47–73; B. Moss and E. Newton, "An examination of the informational text genre in basal readers," *Reading Psychology* 23 (2002): 1–13; M. Pressley, J. Rankin, and L. Yokoi, "A survey of instructional practices of primary teachers nominated as effective in promoting literacy," *Elementary School Journal* 96 (1996): 363–84; Ruth Helen Yopp and Hallie Kay Yopp, "Informational Texts as Read-Alouds in School and Home," *Journal of Literacy Research* 38, no. 1 (2006): 37–51.
6. John T. Guthrie, Amanda Mason-Singh, and Cassandra S. Coddington, "Instructional Effects of Concept-Oriented Reading Instruction on Motivation for Reading Information Text in Middle School," in *Adolescents' Engagement in Academic Literacy,* eds. John T. Guthrie, Allan Wigfield, and Susan Lutz Klauda (College Park, MD: University of Maryland, College Park, 2012), 180.
7. Ibid.
8. Catherine Snow, M. Susan Burns, and Peg Griffin, eds., *Preventing Reading Difficulties in Young Children* (Washington, D.C.: National Academy Press, 1998), 62.
9. L. J. Caswell and Nell K. Duke, "Non-narrative as a catalyst for literacy development," *Language Arts* 75 (1998): 108–17.
10. Miriam J. Dreher, "Motivating struggling readers by tapping the potential of information books," *Reading and Writing Quarterly* 19 (2003): 25–38.
11. Nancy R. Romance and Michael R. Vitale, "Interdisciplinary Perspectives Linking Science and Literacy in Grades K–5: Implications for Policy and Practice," in *Second International Handbook of Science Education,* eds. Barry J. Fraser, Kenneth Tobin, and Campbell J. McRobbie (New York, Springer-Verlag, 2012); Guthrie, Mason-Singh, and Coddington, "Instructional Effects."
12. National Assessment Governing Board, *Reading Framework for the 2011 National Assessment of Educational Progress* (Washington, D.C.: NAGB, Sept. 2010), http://www.nagb.org/content/nagb/assets/documents/publications/frameworks/reading-2011-framework.pdf.
13. National Assessment Governing Board, *Writing Framework for the 2011 National Assessment of Educational Progress* (Washington, D.C.: NAGB, Sept. 2010), http://www.nagb.org/content/nagb/assets/documents/publications/frameworks/writing-2011.pdf.
14. National Governors Association and Council of Chief State School Officers, *Common Core State Standards for English Language Arts and Literacy in History/Social Studies, Science, and Technical Subjects* (Washington, D.C.: NGA and CCSSO, 2010), 5.
15. Ibid.

16. Ibid.
17. Quoted in Dana Goldstein, "The Schoolmaster," *The Atlantic,* Oct. 2012, http://www.theatlantic.com/magazine/archive/2012/10/the-schoolmaster/309091/#.
18. Alexandra Petri, "The Common Core's 70 Percent Nonfiction Standards and the End of Reading?" *Washington Post,* Dec. 7, 2012, http://www.washingtonpost.com/blogs/compost/wp/2012/12/07/the-common-cores-70-percent-nonfiction-standards-and-the-end-of-reading/.
19. Mark Bauerlein and Sandra Stotsky, *How Common Core's ELA Standards Place College Readiness at Risk* (Boston: Pioneer Institute, Sept. 2012).
20. Jennifer McMurrer, *Instructional Time in Elementary Schools: A Closer Look at Changes for Specific Subjects* (Washington, D.C.: Center on Education Policy, Feb. 2008).
21. Catherine Gewertz, "Scales Tip Toward Nonfiction Under the Common Core," *Education Week* 32, no. 12 (Nov. 14, 2012): S15, S16.
22. Cheryl Lederle, *Taking a Closer Look at Presidential Inaugurations: Lincoln's Second Inaugural Address* (Washington, D.C.: Library of Congress, 2013), http://blogs.loc.gov/teachers/2013/01/taking-a-closer-look-at-presidential-inaugurations-lincolns-second-inaugural-address/.
23. Gewertz, "Scales Tip Toward Nonfiction."
24. Ariel Sacks, "Two Common-Core Blunders to Avoid—and How to Do It," *On the Shoulders of Giants,* Aug. 28, 2012, http://teacherleaders.typepad.com/shoulders_of_giants/2012/08/two-common-core-blunders-to-avoid-and-how-to-do-it.html.
25. Carol Jago, "What English Classes Should Look Like in the Common-Core Era," *The Answer Sheet,* Jan. 10, 2013, http://www.washingtonpost.com/blogs/answer-sheet/wp/2013/01/10/what-english-classes-should-look-like-in-common-core-era/.
26. Learning Matters, "What Are Kids Reading?" PBS *NewsHour,* May 14, 2012, http://learningmatters.tv/blog/on-pbs-newshour/watch-what-are-kids-reading/10012/.

Chapter 7

1. Joseph M. Williams and Lawrence McEnerney, *Writing in College: A Short Guide to College Writing* (n.d.) Retrieved from http://writing-program.uchicago.edu/resources/college writing/index.htm.
2. Dana Lundell, Jeanne Higbee, Susan Hipp, and Robert Copeland, *Building Bridges for Access and Success from High School to College: Proceedings of the Metropolitan Higher Education Consortium's Developmental Education Initiative* (Minneapolis, MN: Center for Research on Developmental Education and Urban Literacy, University of Minnesota, 2004).
3. Organisation for Economic Cooperation and Development, *PISA 2009 Results: What Students Know and Can Do* (Paris: OECD, 2010).
4. Daniel T. Willingham, "Critical Thinking: Why Is It So Hard to Teach?" *American Educator* 31, no. 2 (Summer 2007): 8–19.
5. Francine Prose, "Close Reading: Learning to Write by Learning to Read," *The Atlantic,* Aug. 2006, http://www.theatlantic.com/magazine/archive/2006/08/close-reading/305038/.
6. Douglas Fisher and Nancy Frey, *Engaging the Adolescent Learner: Text-Dependent Questions* (Newark, DE: International Reading Association, 2012).
7. Maja Wilson and Thomas Newkirk, "Can Readers Really Stay Within the Standards Lines?" *Education Week* 31, no. 14 (Dec. 14, 2011): 28–29.

8. Catherine Gewertz, "Teachers Embedding Standards in Basal-Reader Questions," *Education Week* 31, no. 30 (Apr. 26, 2012), http://www.edweek.org/ew/articles/2012/04/26/30basal.h31.html.
9. National Center for Educational Statistics, *The Nation's Report Card: Reading 2011* (Washington, D.C.: U.S. Department of Education, NCES, 2011).
10. National Governors Association and Council of Chief State School Officers, *Common Core State Standards for English Language Arts and Literacy in History/Social Studies, Science, and Technical Subjects* (Washington, D.C.: NGA and CCSSO, 2010), 7.
11. Ibid., 10.
12. Ibid., 18.
13. Publishers' criteria.
14. Catherine Gewertz, "Common Standards Ignite Debate over Prereading," *Education Week* 31, no. 29 (Apr. 24, 2012): 1, 22–23; http://www.edweek.org/ew/articles/2012/04/25/29prereading_ep.h31.html?qs=prereading.
15. Sheila Brown and Lee Kappes, *Implementing the Common Core State Standards: A Primer on "Close Reading of Texts"* (Washington, D.C.: Aspen Institute, Oct. 2012), 3.
16. Gewertz, "Common Standards Ignite Debate."
17. Fisher and Frey, *Engaging the Adolescent Learner.*
18. George Hillocks Jr., *Teaching Argument Writing, Grades 6–12* (Portsmouth, NH: Heinemann), xvii.
19. Teaching Channel, "Evidence and Arguments: Lesson Planning," teachingchannel.org; https://www.teachingchannel.org/videos/evidence-arguments-lesson-planning/.
20. Quoted in Catherine Gewertz, "Common Core Thrusts Librarians into Leadership Role," *Education Week* 32, no. 3 (Sept. 12, 2012): 1, 18–19.

Chapter 8

1. L. Drutman, *The Changing Complexity of Congressional Speech* (Washington, D.C.: Sunlight Foundation, 2012).
2. ACT, *Reading Between the Lines: What the ACT Reveals About College Readiness in Reading* (Iowa City, IA: ACT, 2006), 16.
3. Donald P. Hayes, Lorene T. Wolfer, and Michael F. Wolfe, "Schoolbook Simplification and its Relation to the Decline in SAT-Verbal Scores," *American Education Research Journal* 33, no. 2 (1996): 498–508.
4. Ibid.
5. Gary L. Williamson, *Aligning the Journey with a Destination: A Model for K–16 Reading Standards* (Durham, NC: MetaMetrics, Inc., 2006).
6. Kathleen Porter-Magee, "'Just Right' Revisited: 3 Ways We Undermine Student Learning," *Common Core Watch,* June 15, 2012, http://www.edexcellence.net/commentary/education-gadfly-daily/common-core-watch/2012/just-right-books-revisited.html#body.
7. Marilyn J. Adams, "Advancing Our Students' Language and Literacy: The Challenge of Complex Texts," *American Educator* 34, no. 4 (Winter 2010–11): 3–11.
8. Jessica Nelson, Charles Perfetti, David Liben, and Meredith Liben, *Measures of Text Difficulty: Testing Their Predictive Value for Grade Levels and Student Performance* (Washington, D.C.: Council of Chief State School Officers, 2012).
9. Elfrieda H. Hiebert, *The Text Complexity Multi-Index,* http://www.textproject.org/professional-development/text-matters/the-text-complexity-multi-index/.

10. Thomas DeVere Wolsey, Dana L. Grisham, and Elfrieda H. Hiebert, "What Features Influence Text Complexity for Beginning and Struggling Readers?" Text Complexity and the Common Core State Standards, http://www.textproject.org/assets/tds/text-complexity-and-the-ccss/module-3/Module%203-Beginning%20and%20Struggling%20Readers.pdf.
11. http://ell.stanford.edu/sites/default/files/ela_pdf/ELA%20Unit%20Introduction_0.pdf.
12. Lesli A. Maxwell, "N.M. School Builds Bridge to Standards for ELLs," *Education Week* 32, no. 12 (Nov. 14, 2012): S23, S24; http://www.edweek.org/ew/articles/2012/11/14/12cc-ell.h32.html.

Chapter 9

1. Achieve, *Rising to the Challenge: Are High School Graduates Prepared for College and Work?* (Washington, D.C.: Achieve, 2005).
2. Federal Interagency Forum on Child and Family Statistics, *America's Children: Key National Indicators of Well-Being* (Washington, D.C.: U.S. Department of Health and Human Services, 2002).
3. Betty Hart and Todd Risley, *Meaningful Differences in the Everyday Experiences of Young American Children* (Baltimore, MD: Brookes Publishing Company, 1995).
4. Catherine E. Snow, M. Susan Burns, and Peg Griffin, eds., *Preventing Reading Difficulties in Young Children* (Washington, D.C.: National Research Council, 1998).
5. David T. Conley, Katherine V. Drummond, Alicia de Gonzalez, Jennifer Rooseboom, and Odile Stout, *Reaching the Goal: The Applicability and Importance of the Common Core State Standards to College and Career Readiness* (Eugene, OR: University of Oregon, Educational Policy Improvement Center, 2011).
6. Peter D. Hart Research Associates / Public Opinion Strategies, *Rising to the Challenge: Are High School Graduates Prepared for College and Work?* (Washington, D.C.: Achieve, 2005.)
7. Douglas Fisher, Nancy Frey, and Carol Rothenberg, *Content-Area Conversations* (Alexandria, VA: ASCD, 2008).
8. Ibid.
9. Douglas Fisher, Nancy Frey, and Carol Rothenberg, http://www.ascd.org/publications/books/108035/chapters/Why-Talk-Is-Important-in-Classrooms.aspx.
10. Jack C. Richards, *Teaching Listening and Speaking: From Theory to Practice* (Cambridge, UK: Cambridge University Press, 2008).
11. Ibid.
12. Institute for Learning, "Principles of Learning," http://ifl.lrdc.pitt.edu/ifl/index.php/resources/principles_of_learning/.
13. Mortimer J. Adler, *The Paideia Proposal* (New York: Scribner, 1982).
14. National Governors Association and Council of Chief State School Officers, *Common Core State Standards for English Language Arts and Literacy in History/Social Studies, Science, and Technical Subjects* (Washington, D.C.: NGA and CCSSO, 2010), 48.
15. Susan Riddell, "Something to Talk About," *Kentucky Teacher,* May 2012, http://www.kentuckyteacher.org/features/2012/05/something-to-talk-about/.
16. Lancashire County Council, *Assessing Speaking and Listening* (Lancashire, UK: 2010), http://www.lancsngfl.ac.uk/curriculum/assessment/download/file/Key%20Stage%201%20Speaking%20and%20Listening_1.pdf.

Chapter 10

1. Gina Biancarosa and Catherine E. Snow, *Reading Next: A Vision for Action and Research in Middle and High School Literacy.* A Report to Carnegie Corporation of New York (Washington, D.C.: Alliance for Excellent Education, 2006).
2. Catherine E. Snow, M. Susan Burns, and Peg Griffin, eds., *Preventing Reading Difficulties in Young Children* (Washington, D.C.: National Academy Press, 1998), 21.
3. National Center for Education Statistics, *The Nation's Report Card: Reading* (Washington, D.C.: NCES, 2011), http://nationsreportcard.gov/reading_2009/nat_g4.asp?tab_id=tab2&subtab_id=Tab_1#tabsContainer/.
4. National Center for Education Statistics, *The Nation's Report Card: Reading* (Washington, D.C.: NCES, 2009), http://nationsreportcard.gov/reading_2009/gr12_national.asp?tab_id=tab2&subtab_id=Tab_1#tabsContainer/.
5. Beth C. Gamse, Robin Tepper Jacob, Megan Horst, Beth Boulay, and Fatih Unlu, *Reading First Impact Study: Final Report* (Washington, D.C.: U.S. Department of Education, Institute for Education Sciences, Nov. 2008).
6. M. Miller, *Seize the Moment: The Need for a Comprehensive Federal Investment in Adolescent Literacy* (Washington, D.C.: Alliance for Excellent Education, July 2009), 3.
7. Arthur N. Applebee and Judith E. Langer, *The State of Writing Instruction in America's Schools: What the Data Tell Us* (Albany, NY: State University of New York at Albany, 2006).
8. National Center for Education Statistics, *The Nation's Report Card: Writing 2011* (Washington, D.C.: NCES, 2012), http://nces.ed.gov/nationsreportcard/pdf/main2011/2012470.pdf.
9. Rafael Heller and Cynthia L. Greenleaf, *Literacy Instruction in the Content Areas: Getting to the Core of Middle and High School Improvement* (Washington, D.C.: Alliance for Excellent Education, June 2007), 10.
10. Elizabeth Birr Moje, "Foregrounding the Disciplines in Secondary Literacy Teaching and Learning: A Call for Change," *Journal of Adolescent and Adult Literacy* 52, no. 2 (2008): 96–107.
11. National Governors Association and Council of Chief State School Officers, *Common Core State Standards for English Language Arts and Literacy in History/Social Studies, Science, and Technical Subjects* (Washington, D.C.: NGA and CCSSO, 2010), 60.
12. Eric Robelen, "Literacy Instruction Expected to Cross Disciplines," *Education Week* 32, no. 12 (Nov. 14, 2012): S18, S19, S20; http://www.edweek.org/ew/articles/2012/11/14/12cc-crosscurriculum.h32.html?qs=Common+Core+literacy+science/.
13. Ibid.
14. Quoted in ibid.
15. Catherine Gewertz, "Reading on Science, Social Studies Teachers' Agendas," *Education Week* 31, no. 29 (Apr. 25, 2012): S18, S20, S21, S22, S23.
16. Ibid.
17. National Research Council, *A Framework for K–12 Science Education: Practices, Crosscutting Concepts, and Core Ideas* (Washington, D.C.: National Academies Press, 2011).

18. Helen Quinn, Okhee Lee, and Guadalupe Valdés, *Language Demands and Opportunities in Relation to the Next Generation Science Standards: What Teachers Need to Know* (Palo Alto, CA: Stanford University, 2012), 3.
19. Ibid., 7.

Chapter 11

1. James Spillane, *Standards Deviation: How Schools Misunderstand Education Policy* (Cambridge, MA: Harvard University Press, 2004).
2. Nancy Kober and Diane Stark Rentner, *Year Two of Implementing the Common Core State Standards: Progress and Challenges* (Washington, D.C.: Center on Education Policy, 2012).
3. William Porter, Regina Riley, Lisa Towne, Sean M. Chalk, Amy Hightower, Sterling C. Lord, Carrie A. Matthews, and Christopher B. Swanson, *Moving Forward: A National Perspective on States' Progress in Common Core State Standards Implementation Planning* (Seattle and Bethesda, MD: Education First and Editorial Projects in Education, Feb. 2013).
4. Accountability Works, *National Cost of Aligning States and Localities to the Common Core Standards* (Boston: Pioneer Institute, 2012).
5. P. J. Murphy and E. Regenstein, *Putting a Price Tag on the Common Core: How Much Will Smart Implementation Cost?* (Washington, D.C.: Thomas B. Fordham Institute. 2012), http://edexcellencemedia.net/publications/2012/20120530-Putting-A-Price-Tag-on-the-Common-Core/20120530-Putting-a-Price-Tag-on-the-Common-Core-FINAL.pdf.
6. Brian Stecher and Hilda Borko, *Combining Surveys and Case Studies to Examine Standards-Based Education Reform*, CSE Technical Report 565 (Los Angeles: University of California, Los Angeles, National Center for Research on Evaluation, Standards, and Student Testing, 2002).
7. Matthew M. Chingos, *Strength in Numbers: State Spending on K–12 Assessment Systems* (Washington, D.C.: Brookings Institution, Nov. 2012).
8. Barry Topol, John Olson, and Ed Roeber, *The Cost of New Higher-Quality Assessments: A Comprehensive Analysis of the Potential Costs of Future State Assessments* (Stanford, CA: Stanford Center for Opportunity Policy in Education, 2010).
9. Catherine Gewertz, "Testing Group Scales Back Performance Items," *Education Week*, Nov. 29, 2012, http://www.edweek.org/ew/articles/2012/11/30/13tests.h32.html?tkn=OYTFHGT9CFHlsM2VveoLDPuR1m0hNwKtk7ID&cmp=clp-edweek/.
10. Achieve, *Growing Awareness, Growing Support: Teacher and Voter Understanding of the Common Core Standards and Assessments* (Washington, D.C.: Achieve, June 2012).
11. American Federation of Teachers, "AFT Calls for Moratorium on High-Stakes Consequences of Common-Core Tests," Press Release, Apr. 30, 2013.

Acknowledgments

This book emerged from a short online article for the *Harvard Education Letter* in August 2012. I am grateful for the help and support of many people who enabled me to turn it out so quickly.

Thanks first to my colleagues at the Alliance for Excellent Education, especially Bob Wise and Elizabeth Schneider, for their encouragement and support. They have done much to make the Common Core Standards a reality, and I am proud to work with them. While this book was written outside of my formal duties at the Alliance, they have cheered me on and have been generous with advice and knowledge.

I am also grateful to Sue Pimentel and Jason Zimba, lead authors of the Standards, who were generous with their time in sharing background on the Standards. Sue also went the extra mile and commented on draft chapters, as did her colleagues at Student Achievement Partners, David Liben and Emily Climer, and I thank them for it. Any remaining errors are mine. I also thank Joanna Hawkins for providing examples of student essays.

This book would not have happened without the strong encouragement and support of Nancy Walser of Harvard Education Press, who saw the seeds of a volume in the short *HEL* article and saw it through to publication. I am proud to be associated with Nancy and her colleagues.

I also owe a debt of gratitude, once again, to my wife, Karla Winters, and my daughter, Cleo Rothman, for putting up with my night and weekend work. I dedicate this to them.

About the Author

Robert Rothman is a senior fellow at the Alliance for Excellent Education, a Washington, D.C.–based policy and advocacy organization. Previously he was a senior editor at the Annenberg Institute for School Reform, where he edited the Institute's quarterly magazine, *Voices in Urban Education.* He was also a study director at the National Research Council, where he led a committee on testing and assessment in the federal Title I program, which produced the report *Testing, Teaching, and Learning* (edited with Richard F. Elmore), as well as a committee on teacher testing. A nationally known education writer and editor, Mr. Rothman has also worked with Achieve and the National Center on Education and the Economy, and was a reporter and editor for *Education Week.* He has written numerous reports and articles on a wide range of education issues. He is the author of *Something in Common: The Common Core Standards and the Next Chapter in American Education* (2011) and *Measuring Up: Standards, Assessments and School Reform* (1995), and he is the editor of *City Schools* (2007). He is also a frequent contributor to *Harvard Education Letter.* Mr. Rothman holds a degree in political science from Yale University.

Index